HOW TO REMOVE
TRAUMA
RESPONSE

A Memory
Reconsolidation
Guidebook for
Therapists
and Coaches

ALUN PARRY

How To Remove Trauma Response : A Memory Reconsolidation Guidebook for Therapists and Coaches

First Printing, 2022

ISBN : 978-1-3999-3360-5

Published by FRESH Therapists

Addresses for FRESH Therapists can be found at
freshtherapists.com/address
FRESH Therapists
freshtherapists.com

Cover design by: Lemondrop Creative
Book Interior and E-book Design by Amit Dey | amitdey2528@gmail.com

"The new approach Alun shared with me is fast, quick and easy. It's really helpful. I was dubious to start with, and now I'm a real advocate of it. It really works."

— Sandra Burlace, Psychotherapist

"Alun taught me some of his ideas on how to apply memory reconsolidation. Soon after, I tried them with a client I was working with. She described the session as 'transformational' and it had a real impact on her life."

— Louise Bellamy, Psychotherapist

"Alun Parry is doing a great job of synthesising trauma-focused therapeutic approaches and passing on his know-how to other therapists. As well as offering regular online tutorials, Alun also goes the extra mile in providing personalised responses to the members of his coaching group. An example of this was a very detailed answer to a question I had regarding a therapy client with social anxiety.

I have also learned from Alun:

- The importance of the Autonomic Nervous System response, and how to see this as a sign of the "core prediction", or the part of the client's psyche that yells STOP!
- Selecting from a variety of possible therapeutic approaches to deepen the discovery work and help the client to notice how the core prediction turns up in their life.

- Triggering memory reconsolidation of these old patterns through imagined experiences."

— Kevan Owen, Counsellor & Psychotherapist

"Learning memory reconsolidation has had a significant impact on my practice. It's very rewarding when you help a client resolve a long-standing issue and they're surprised because the process is very quick and non-intrusive. Two clients initially didn't believe the issues had been resolved because it seemed too easy, but they had."

— Byron Athene, Counselling Psychotherapist

CONTENTS

INTRODUCTION

The eye has a mechanism that changes the size of your pupils. Point a flashlight in your eyes and the pupils go smaller. Move into a dark room, they grow big. It's a biological mechanism and is a natural way that the eye works.

The brain has biological mechanisms too. One of them is called memory reconsolidation. It doesn't change the size of your pupils. It erases trauma. Completely. So it's gone for good. This is a natural way that the brain works.

Neuroscientists only discovered it in the late 90s. I found out about it by accident, at the back end of a chance conversation.

I don't want you to find out about it by chance. It's too important for that. So, I've written this book.

Working with memory reconsolidation has changed my life, my work, and my therapy practice.

Better still, it has changed the lives of many of my clients who were living with the effects of trauma.

They were once expected to manage their trauma. Now, it is gone completely.

They don't relapse. When this brain mechanism is triggered, it wipes the trauma so it is no longer there. You can't activate non-existent trauma.

It may sound magical, but it's real. We now know the exact steps that the brain needs to trigger it.

As therapists, we simply need to map our approach to these steps.

It means we can erase trauma responses reliably and predictably just by giving the brain what it needs.

In this book, I'm going to show you what the brain needs to naturally erase trauma.

I'll also show you some approaches and why they work.

You'll learn how to evaluate and tweak therapies so they map what the brain needs, rather than miss it.

CHAPTER 1

HOW TO USE THIS BOOK

This book is intended for therapists, counsellors and coaches who work with, or hope to work with, the effects of trauma. In particular, it covers a discovery in neuroscience. This discovery identified a brain mechanism that literally erases the trauma response.

Neuroscience discoveries are interesting and exciting. Yet, the real question for therapists like ourselves is: how do we make use of them in the therapy room?

This book is designed to introduce you to this revolutionary discovery, and show you how to create this transformation reliably.

Although aimed as a handbook for therapists, clients are welcome to read this book too. It will show you that real change is possible. The science says so. Trauma is no longer something to be managed or befriended. It can now be gotten rid of for good.

The book is divided into three sections. The first outlines what the neuroscience discovery is. It looks at the implications of the discovery. It shows how what we think of therapy can now move into a fresh paradigm - one where relapse is no longer possible.

The second section lists the seven steps of transformational change. It provides a road map for how to trigger the brain mechanism that removes trauma. It is, in essence, a step-by-step guide to the erasure of trauma, along with examples.

The final section looks at imaginal approaches for triggering this brain mechanism. Given that this is a biological brain mechanism rather than a model, there are many ways we can trigger it as therapists. Once we know the seven steps, we can be as creative and inventive as we need to be. Imaginal work is an example of how to go beyond words in order to create transformation.

Why This Book

There are many books about psychotherapy. There are even books about trauma. So why would I decide to add another to the volume?

The key reason is that I noticed most therapists don't seem to know about memory reconsolidation. I say this without any criticism implied. As you'll see in a moment, I found out about it by accident myself.

Whenever I mention this brain mechanism called memory reconsolidation, my colleagues and friends don't know what it is. Despite the implications of this discovery, word is getting around slowly. This book is part of my attempt to share the good news.

My own introduction to memory reconsolidation was an accident. A therapist from out of town moved to my region and, to get to know some local colleagues, reached out to me for a conversation. I agreed and we chatted about many different topics.

Almost as an afterthought, near the end of our chat she asked: "Have you heard about memory reconsolidation?"

I hadn't. When she told me a little more about it, it was the start of a rabbit hole that I was about to venture into. I was eager to discover how it worked and how I could help my clients with it.

Since then, my studies have led me to being able to reliably trigger this brain mechanism with my clients. The effect has been revolutionary. Clients I had been struggling to help suddenly had their trauma responses erased. Problems they seemed stuck with are gone.

Most incredibly, these include responses that they have no conscious control over. Involuntary responses like blushing no longer occur. Such is the power of memory reconsolidation to physically erase the responses of trauma.

As you are reading this, you may feel some skepticism. This is more than understandable. Even while working with clients, there is a voice in my own head telling me that this can't possibly work. But of course it does. It may seem miraculous. I get that. It does to me, too, and to my clients.

But it's not a miracle. It is neuroscience. When we understand the lessons of neuroscience and follow the steps of memory reconsolidation, we can trigger these miracles reliably.

This discovery and its application has revolutionised my therapy work. I may have discovered it through a chance conversation. But it is far too important to be shared by chance. Through this book, I want to pass on the power of memory reconsolidation so it can benefit you and your clients.

We are therapists because we want to help people. We want their lives to be free of the impacts of the worse things that happen to them. We want to set them free of their past. The discovery of this brain mechanism shows us exactly how.

About Me

So who am I to be writing such a book?

First of all, I'll tell you who I am not. I'm not a neuroscientist. This book covers a discovery in neuroscience. Yet the aim of this book is to help you apply its findings.

As such, I won't be digging too deep into the workings of the brain, or even to get too into the weeds on the various experiments. My aim is not to write a scientific paper, but a practical guide.

I will be looking at aspects of the brain, but on a minimum dose basis. If I don't need to talk about it, I won't. I'll tell you what you need to know in order to understand it and apply its lessons.

As a therapist, my goal is to pass on this knowledge in such a way that my colleagues can begin applying this discovery in practice with clients in the therapy room.

This book is an introduction to the topic. There is plenty more to discuss regarding memory reconsolidation. I could write an enormous volume. But that would be less helpful.

Instead, I chose to write something concise that gives you the core knowledge as quickly as possible.

Now that I've told you I'm not a neuroscientist, I'll tell you who I am. I am a psychotherapist based in the North West of England in the UK. I specialise in working with adults who still suffer the impact of childhood trauma. Often, with such clients, their trauma was repeated. For instance, they may have grown up witnessing domestic violence. As such, this trauma repeats throughout their childhood rather than it being a singular, one-off event.

I am also the founder of FRESHTherapists.com. This is a website and training resource. It translates the science of transformation into something that fellow therapists can put into action.

Bonus Resources

I have created a range of additional resources to help you remember and apply this book in your client work. To get these bonus resources, visit removetrauma.com

To read lots of free articles on this topic, visit FRESHTherapists.com where you can be trained by me personally.

You can also sign up to my FRESHTherapists newsletter to hear first about new articles and trainings.

You may like to join my Memory Reconsolidation Coaching Academy. This is exclusively for therapists and coaches who wish to be experts at removing trauma. You can find out more at FRESHTherapists.com/coaching

Trauma and Trauma Response – Some Definitions

This book shows therapists how to literally erase trauma response. Some definitions would be helpful. What is trauma? What do I mean by responses to trauma?

There are many definitions of trauma. There are plenty of debates around what counts as trauma too. Some like to divide the topic of trauma into 'big T' and 'little t' trauma.

For therapists seeking to trigger memory reconsolidation, these distinctions are not so relevant.

When I refer to trauma in this book, know that I am using this definition:

"A psychological injury that was significant enough to still be touching your life today."

This broad definition is helpful because it steps away from the risk of minimising someone's pain by categorising it as a less significant trauma.

More importantly, the brain mechanism works on anything that fits this broad definition, so there is no benefit to such limitations.

Now that trauma is defined, what do I mean by a trauma response? I see a trauma response as the beliefs and nervous system responses that ensured you survived this traumatic event.

For example, the little boy who was beaten for laughing too loudly may decide to stay quiet or never laugh. Now grown, he still instinctively uses this strategy. It ensured he survived back then, so can be regarded as a trauma response. Indeed, this might be the very issue that brought him to therapy.

Another example is the little girl who was ridiculed by her parents and may decide to believe that she is defective in some way. Perhaps believing that her parents were the problem was too scary for a child who still depended on them. Maybe she figured that blaming herself gave her more power to solve the problem than hoping others change. This sense of self defectiveness can also be viewed as a trauma response. She may come for therapy with an issue that is linked to this sense of self worth.

Trauma responses are also the way the body reacts when now resembles back then. Let us revisit the little boy above. Think of him as a grown man being invited to be big and loud. His nervous system would sense danger and so trigger a nervous system response that is felt in the body. These reactions are involuntary and form part of a trauma response.

Memory Reconsolidation

In the next section of the book, we will look at the discovery of memory reconsolidation itself and why it is important.

You will understand what memory reconsolidation is and how it works. You will appreciate how it is different from what neuroscience previously believed. You will see that this discovery ushers in a whole new paradigm of doing therapy itself.

You will also understand why clients relapse. Moreover, you will see why therapy that triggers memory reconsolidation makes relapse literally impossible. It's a bold claim, but also true, as you will soon find out.

PART ONE

THE DISCOVERY

CHAPTER 2

WHAT IS MEMORY RECONSOLIDATION?

Memory reconsolidation is a brain mechanism. In other words, it happens physiologically in the brain. It is not another psychological theory, but a biological fact.

It was first discovered in 1997. Before that date, neuroscientists believed that the brain worked differently. That belief had an impact on therapy itself.

Memory reconsolidation is the only known brain mechanism that results in transformational change. Pay special attention to the word "only". It holds a huge significance. I shall return to that in a moment.

But first, what do I mean by "transformational change"?

There are various types of change. For instance, we can modify our behaviour for a short while before slipping back to old ways again. We all experience this at the start of each year. We call them New Year's Resolutions.

Every gym member will tell you that the gyms fill up in January and are empty again in February.

Some changes last longer, but still result in returning to our old ways.

Other changes are longer lasting but depend on us "doing the work". As long as we keep disciplined and do the work, we can maintain the changes. It's an effort. We have to keep showing up. But so long as we do, we can maintain the changes.

These are all examples of change. But they are not what I refer to as transformational change.

Transformational change has two identifying characteristics.

First, it is permanent. That means that unlike those New Year's Resolutions, we don't slip back into our old ways. In fact, truly transformational change means that such a relapse is not possible.

Admittedly, this is a high bar. But given what neuroscience has learned about the brain mechanism of memory reconsolidation, we should be aiming for it. In the coming pages, you will understand why such a goal is not at all outlandish but can be the typical outcome of psychotherapy.

Secondly, the change is effortless to maintain. The client doesn't need to keep showing up or devoting their energies to exercises or habits to keep on track.

Think of anything you have always done effortlessly. Maybe you notice that a friend gets hot and bothered about public speaking whereas you don't in the slightest. Use whatever example fits you best.

It's not that you feel calm about it because of the work you do every day. No, you are just calm about it. Your nervous system has a different response to the one your friend has.

Transformational change brings about that same level of ease. You don't think about it, even though it used to be very triggering. Now, it's simply not a problem.

In other words, it is as if you never experienced trauma at all.

This is the goal for our clients. Not because we are being overly ambitious or setting ourselves and our clients up to fail. But because neuroscience tells us that we can. Moreover, it gives us the exact steps on how to achieve it reliably.

Now that we know that this brain mechanism exists, how can we aim any lower?

The Only Known Mechanism of Trauma Removal

I pointed out earlier that memory reconsolidation is the only known brain mechanism that creates transformational change.

The implication of this is significant. It means that it is the reason why any such transformation ever occurs.

It is, in effect, the only door to the room. Think of a room that has no windows or secret passages, and the only way in is through one door. It follows that anyone who is in the room must have entered through that door.

Likewise, any time a client experiences transformational change of the kind described, it follows that memory reconsolidation has occurred. Why? Because it is the only brain mechanism that can achieve it.

Think of all the various methods, techniques, and modalities that produce transformational change. They must, in their own way, be triggering this brain mechanism.

Think of your own clients who have experienced the kind of change that is permanent and effortless to maintain. Memory reconsolidation must have occurred for them too.

Therapists do trigger memory reconsolidation, even without knowing it exists. As you learn more about it, you will realise how therapists have intuitively moved into the right areas.

Yet, memory reconsolidation does have specific steps to follow. Once we learn what they are, we know exactly how to trigger it. As a result, we can make sure we do. We move from triggering it sometimes to triggering it reliably.

Our potency as therapists increases. Our clients get the life changes they want.

A Mechanism – Not A Modality

The idea that this is the only way to trigger such a change may produce a reaction. So many times in psychotherapy's history, there have been those who argued that their method was the only way to create change.

Such claims can invite charges of monotheism.

These concerns are valid. Let me reassure you. Memory reconsolidation is not a method at all. It is simply a description of what happens in the brain to allow it to overwrite trauma responses. It is a description of a biological brain mechanism.

Rather than closing down the field to one particular approach, it raises a more interesting possibility. It allows many different approaches.

Think of a journey you may wish to take. You have a destination in mind, say a friend's house. You will, of course, need to enter your friend's street and you will have to get to your friend's front door.

But isn't everything else completely up for grabs?

You could cycle there. You could get on the train. You could drive. You could get a taxi. You could walk. You could mix it up by cycling to the train station, taking the train, and then cycling the rest of the way to your friend.

You could take a direct route or you could take a scenic route. Maybe several scenic routes are on offer, so you can choose which.

As long as you end up on your friend's street and reach your friend's front door, all journeys are valid.

Memory reconsolidation is the same. It offers a road map of the steps that the brain needs. But the way you travel is up to you.

It means you can use your current modality, perhaps with some tweaks that make it even more effective. You can create a whole new way of working entirely. You can even decide to mix and match, depending on the preferences of your client.

So long as you find a way to follow the crucial steps that trigger memory reconsolidation, you don't need to practice in a uniform way at all.

It opens up possibilities rather than closes them down. It encourages experimentation, creativity, and difference.

Indeed, it is likely that memory reconsolidation is an element that explains common factors theory. Common factors theory notes that hundreds of different modalities get very similar client outcomes. So, it presupposes that there must be aspects of therapy that are held in common. Wherever there is permanent, effortless change, memory reconsolidation is the aspect held in common.

This can free you up as a therapist rather than constrain you. Once you know the steps of memory reconsolidation, you will see the innovation and difference that it encourages.

Memory reconsolidation is a biological brain mechanism. The model you choose is your vehicle for getting there.

A Framework for Therapist Self Reflection

The knowledge that this brain mechanism exists allows for powerful reflections about our work. Self-reflection is a key part of any therapist's work. Now we can do it in a way that is more focused on achieving results for our clients.

For instance, we can reflect on our successes with clients in a way that appreciates how change takes place. We can think of a client who achieved lasting change and identify how we triggered the brain mechanism of memory reconsolidation.

Simply knowing the required steps allows us to think back to any client who experienced this change and learn from those successes. We can map the steps to our past work and understand how the change occurred.

In this way, we can generate methods of practice that reliably create that change again. It moves us from having a vague idea of what we did well to specifically mapping how we met the steps of memory reconsolidation.

The benefit is that once we understand what works and why, we can do it again and again. This improves you as a practitioner. It also achieves better outcomes for your clients as you do more of what works with a genuine appreciation of why.

This makes deliberate practice more achievable too. There are many in our field who champion deliberate practice as a way to become better therapists. They highlight the 10,000 hours rule of deliberate practice that Anders Ericsson writes about in his study of expertise.

The problem with the idea of deliberate practice is that it applies best to mechanical, repeatable tasks. A guitarist learning scales, for instance. With psychotherapy, it is not so clear. What is the equivalent in our field for repeatedly pressing your finger on a particular string in the right way?

There are specific steps needed for memory reconsolidation. It doesn't quite make it akin to a guitarist learning scales. But it does identify more clearly the aspects of work that we need to get good at.

Knowing the steps of memory reconsolidation turbocharges our reflections about our work. It gives us a framework for reflecting on our work. It helps us understand why we are successful when we are. As such, we can do it more. We become more confident and more effective as therapists.

A License for Creativity

Some clients prefer to talk. Others find it hard to talk and prefer to do movement. Others enjoy expressing themselves through artwork and creativity. Other clients like imaginal exercises.

Some want to delve into the past. Others prefer to stay in the present. Some prefer one way of conceptualising their issue. Others connect better to another way of thinking about them. Some clients are spiritual. Some are very pragmatic.

This is only the tip of the iceberg. There are many differences in the needs and preferences of clients.

If there was only one way to do psychotherapy, it would miss the majority of the population.

When you learn a new modality, it can sometimes imply a rejection of other modalities. You used to do psychotherapy that way. Now you should do it this way - the "right" way.

Yet, different therapists use different modalities and get results for their clients. How can there be a "right" way if many of the "wrong" ways work too? Memory reconsolidation has nothing to say about approaches and modalities. Just as a map has nothing to say about your mode of transport. The neuroscience simply tells us which steps the brain needs so that memory reconsolidation occurs.

If you hit those beats, it happens. How you hit those beats is up to you and your clients. When you know what those beats are, you can reliably create transformative, lasting change with your clients, irrespective of your modality.

If you have a way of working that works for you, don't worry. Learning the steps of memory reconsolidation does not mean that you have to abandon how you currently work. It will just make your approach more effective. You may tweak it. But the fundamental approach can stay as it is.

As you get more familiar with the steps of memory reconsolidation, you may notice that you become more creative. You understand why change happens. You begin to see possibilities that were hidden when you were stuck within the teachings of a modality.

You may find yourself, as I have, developing brand new approaches that fit the steps of memory reconsolidation.

You will notice yourself stripping away the fat from models already out there. You'll feel permitted to borrow aspects from them more. You will no longer believe that you must learn the whole approach. Instead, you notice which aspects fit with memory reconsolidation. You swipe those and apply them successfully.

Your learning speeds up. Your potency and range as a therapist magnifies. The sense you sometimes have of feeling lost lessens. You feel like you always have a road map, no matter what the client brings.

You always feel confident that you can help because you know that transformational change is possible, and you know the steps needed to get there.

Your ability to improvise increases and adds to your confidence. You end up quickly developing a range of techniques and approaches without the steep learning curve that usually comes with learning.

Creativity now comes naturally. You enjoy your work as a therapist more than ever.

You Have Already Done It

Think of any client who experienced this kind of transformational change. Change lasted and was effortless for them. Whatever you did together triggered memory reconsolidation. After all, it is the only known brain mechanism that can create this kind of change.

So, if you think back across your cases and find a client who fits that description, you've already done this.

Given that you've already done this, you don't have to learn how to do it. You only need to learn how to do it reliably and consistently.

The steps of memory reconsolidation will show you how to keep getting that outcome. But your successes so far show you that you are already in the right area.

Imagine hitting the wall in a particular part of the room. As you reach around the wall, pushing and hitting, the light eventually comes on. It's a testament to your brilliance that you found yourself in the right area of the wall.

But once someone tells you what a light switch is, the light goes on every time and faster too.

In the same way, learning memory reconsolidation refines what you already do so that you can do it reliably - and more quickly.

You have already created transformational change. You will no doubt do it again, even if you close this book and never read another word. What you are learning here is how to do it consistently.

In the following chapters, you will find out what has changed in the world of neuroscience as a result of the discovery of memory reconsolidation. You will learn how revolutionary that is for us as psychotherapists, and, most importantly, for the clients we serve.

CHAPTER 3

THE BREAKTHROUGH IN NEUROSCIENCE

B race yourself. This is the part of the book where we have to discuss neuroscience. My intention is to be as quick as possible. I will limit explanations to what we need to know to understand why this is an important breakthrough. Then we can switch focus to how it impacts therapists and therapy.

The first thing that we need to understand is what happens in the brain itself when a traumatic event occurs. The brain encodes our responses onto an actual brain pathway. This pathway physically exists within the brain. As such, trauma responses are written anatomically into a real physical location.

In the future, whenever something occurs that resembles the trauma, the brain predicts that these responses are needed once more. It goes back to that particular brain pathway and plays out the instructions that are encoded there.

For instance, the person may notice that their nervous system has activated and they are in the midst of an anxiety attack.

The same response that was encoded onto that brain pathway all those years ago is replayed at this moment.

The key question is: can these brain pathways be rewritten, or are these trauma responses permanent?

Until recently, it was believed that brain pathways containing a traumatic response were locked forever. They could not be rewritten or changed. If we endured a traumatic event, we were stuck with those responses for the rest of our lives.

This seemed reasonable, especially from an evolutionary point of view. If we experience something threatening or highly emotionally significant, the brain wants us to remember it.

If you forget to respond to the rustling of a tree and it is often a lion that causes that rustling, you won't last very long. The brain does not want us to forget our responses to such existential information.

Yet with trauma responses, they trigger even when the old danger is gone. Some cue in the present may merely resemble the event back then and cause the trauma to resurface.

The nervous system's power kicks in and stops us from doing all sorts of things we want to do. Not because we are unsafe now, but because these responses kept us safe back then.

It moves from being a vital resource to an outdated hindrance. It would be helpful to be able to update these responses. Once updated, the client's suffering would be removed and they could live the life they want instead.

Yet neuroscientists believed that brain pathways containing these vital trauma responses could never be changed, even to update their learning.

We now know that this is not true. Instead, the brain does allow these pathways to be rewritten, but not easily. It will do so only under specific circumstances.

The brain still wants us to hold on strongly to those traumatic responses that helped us survive danger. It wants us to remember how to respond to a lion. But the way it protects that learning is different from how we once believed.

We now know that it protects such learning much like a combination safe. A combination safe offers robust protection and is not easily accessed. However, if you know the right steps to take, the safe will open, and the contents can be changed.

This is how trauma-encoded brain pathways work too.

The brain keeps significant learning protected. But it will allow this old learning to be rewritten and updated too. We just need to know the correct steps to open that door.

With memory reconsolidation, neuroscientists have laid out the steps that the brain needs to be able to do this.

As therapists, this is groundbreaking information. For the first time, the steps by which transformational change can occur are set out for us.

This breakthrough in our understanding of how the brain works has implications for therapy itself.

It offers a brand new way of thinking about therapeutic change. The old paradigm could only compete with trauma. The new paradigm promises erasure. It allows for a level of healing that neuroscience once thought impossible.

Competitive Therapy in the Brain

As therapists, we don't often think about what is going on biologically in the brain. We are working directly with the person. But there is a brain process going on nonetheless.

Neuroscience once told us that our clients are stuck with the old trauma response, and it could not be changed.

In that case, our only option was to build a new brain pathway to store the response the client wants instead.

This is the old paradigm of competitive style therapy. We are stuck with the old trauma, so we'll create a new pathway to compete with it.

Over weeks and maybe years of therapy, this brain pathway is built and nurtured. The work strengthens the new pathway and helps the client to be more capable of choosing it.

As time moves on, even though the old brain pathway's trauma responses remain, the client increasingly uses the new, healthy option. Whereas once they followed one path on autopilot, they now experience themself as facing a crossroads.

By increasingly choosing the new brain pathway and its healthy responses, the client's life changes for the better. The more they choose the new brain pathway, the stronger it gets.

The old brain trauma response is still there. But the client is no longer choosing it. Life improves. Despite being stuck with the old trauma response, change happens anyhow.

This is competitive therapy. It says to the old, supposedly unchangeable brain pathway, "I can't change you, so I'll create something to compete with you."

So, What's the Problem?

As you can see, this method does indeed work. It does produce change and many people's lives have improved as a result of it. So, what's the problem?

The problem is the same as any competition. Winning is not guaranteed.

Have you ever worked with a client, their life has changed, and they leave happy and grateful? You feel good about yourself and you are really satisfied with the work. They are consistently making those new choices in their life and are able to end therapy.

And then, several months later, you get a call. Things are back to where they started. They need your help again.

This can be so dispiriting to both the client and the therapist. The client loses hope. Even when life begins to improve again, they hold a doubt that it is temporary. Soon, the old way of being hits them all over again.

This is what we call relapse, and it happens for a very good reason.

In competitive therapy, the old brain pathway with all of the old patterns and responses still exists.

It's like being in charge of the town bridges and waking up one morning to learn that a car took the old rickety bridge and is now in the river.

The old trauma responses were developed at times of scare or threat. The aim of these responses was to keep the client safe during this time. They worked, because the client is here talking to you.

When life becomes super stressful, it is a strong invite to the old brain pathway to trigger its responses. The more the stress, the bigger the invite, because the situation seems more threatening and challenging to your client.

Why wouldn't the brain use the tried and trusted approach and revert to that old brain pathway, with those proven trauma responses?

They may not be that helpful in this particular situation. In fact, they may now be an outright hindrance.

But the old brain pathway with its old trauma response is still there to be used. When it is, the client suffers relapse. The suffering they sought help with returns.

As with any competition, you can lose. In relapse, the new brain pathway, containing healthy desired responses, loses out to the old brain pathway with its trauma response.

Relapse is only possible because overwriting that brain pathway wasn't considered an option. If only there was a way to erase it, relapse could never again happen. The brain could choose that tried and trusted brain pathway, but the contents would now be different.

Erasure Therapy

Remember the metaphor of the combination safe. This is our new understanding of how the brain works.

We now have a better option than competitive therapy. Competitive therapy is an ingenious response if we think we are stuck with our trauma response forever.

But that understanding has changed. We now know that we are not stuck with that trauma response forever. Like a safe, it may need precise steps, but we can change the contents of that brain pathway.

Think of an audio cassette tape of the kind that were once commonplace until the 1990s. Imagine you are going on a road trip and you have a cassette with awful music on.

The last thing you want to do is play that cassette on your trip and listen to those terrible tunes for the whole journey.

One option may be the competitive therapy approach. You keep the old cassette, but you bring another one with great music. When faced with the choice of playing the lousy cassette or the enjoyable one, you put the enjoyable cassette on.

Except you have a partner on the trip, and they just love that lousy music. It's their favourite. They see the old tape and their eyes light up. They turn out to be pretty persuasive, so guess what you're listening to on that trip? Ugghh!

The erasure therapy approach wouldn't risk that. Instead, you'd record over the lousy music. Now you just have the one cassette tape and the music on it is awesome!

When your persuasive friend gets in the car and plays that old cassette, their awful music has been wiped. It may be the same cassette tape, but the contents are now to your liking.

This is erasure therapy, but applied to brain pathways and trauma response. The brain pathway is the cassette. The trauma response is the music on it.

There is no need to create new brain pathways to compete with the old. Instead, you can erase and rewrite the one you already have.

The benefit is that, even under immense stress, when the brain triggers that old brain pathway, the trauma response is gone.

The End of Relapse

Have you ever worked with a client and, after some time, they reach a point where they are ready to end therapy? The issue they brought is now sorted and they are enjoying life. It's a joyous moment. These are the kind of moments that make being a therapist so meaningful.

Then three months later they are back - with the exact same problem.

Erasure therapy means that can never happen. With erasure therapy, your job is to trigger the brain mechanism of memory reconsolidation. When that happens, the brain pathway is overwritten and updated.

Like the cassette tape, the old is simply no longer present. The brain still heads to the same old brain pathway. But its contents are now to your client's liking.

This makes relapse impossible. Those old trauma responses are simply not there.

The old paradigm left the door wide open for relapse. The way of memory reconsolidation means that relapse is no longer even available. Relapse is as impossible as hearing the lousy music on the cassette tape you recorded over.

With memory reconsolidation, the change is permanent. Its permanence means that no effort is needed from your client. No homework. No daily exercises to keep the problem at bay. They live without the trauma response as if they had never had a trauma response.

Erasure means it has been erased. It can never return. It heralds the end of relapse.

A Quick Recap

Let's have a quick recap on what you have learned so far.

Neuroscientists used to think that brain pathways containing trauma responses were locked forever. It was thought impossible to rewrite them, so as to protect the learning.

We now know that the brain is protective of that learning in a more flexible way. It wants to protect it, yet be able to update that learning too. As such, it works more like a combination safe.

It's not like a cupboard, which is easy to open and change the contents. Instead, there are specific steps needed to open the safe.

Brain pathways containing trauma response can open, but we need to take specific steps to open them. We need to know the combination to the lock. In the next section of this book, I will describe what those steps are so that you, too, will know how to update and erase trauma.

Once you know them, you will be able to work with clients in such a way as to literally erase unhelpful trauma responses. Once those are gone, they can not return. Relapse becomes not just unlikely, but impossible.

CHAPTER 4

THE ETERNAL SUNSHINE OF THE SPOTLESS MIND?

In the 2004 movie *The Eternal Sunshine of the Spotless Mind*, Jim Carrey and Kate Winslet play a couple who have a beautiful relationship. Sadly, the relationship turns sour. They each undergo a medical procedure to erase the other from their memories. They no longer know that the other even existed, and they don't remember anything about their relationship at all.

Given that memory reconsolidation literally erases trauma, you may well be wondering if this is what happens here.

Will your client leave therapy with whole chunks of their history and memory erased? Will they no longer even know that the bad thing happened to them at all? What are the ethics of a client no longer even knowing their own story anymore?

It's an interesting ethical question. Yet, thankfully, it's one that we don't need to consider because this is not the outcome of memory reconsolidation.

Indeed, the term memory reconsolidation is somewhat imprecise because there are different types of memory systems.

What Do We Mean by Memory?

There are many kinds of memory that are operated by completely different parts of the brain.

First, there is working memory. In computing terms, this is our equivalent to RAM. It allows us to hold information temporarily. The prefrontal cortex is the part of the brain that is involved with working memory.

Working memory is not erased when memory reconsolidation is triggered.

Another kind is episodic memory. I often refer to this as story memory. It is the memory you call upon when relating an episode from your life. When you tell a story to a friend, for instance, you call upon episodic memory. A different part of the brain is used to hold and tell these stories, called the hippocampus.

Episodic memory is not erased when memory reconsolidation is triggered. (Interestingly, the brain seems quite relaxed about story details and does not hold on to them too tightly. Memory studies show that as much as 50% of the details of any story are altered over time - not because the person is lying, but because the brain does not care so much about these details.)

So, if working memory and story memory remain untouched by memory reconsolidation, what kind of memory is erased?

The answer is implicit memory. There are two parts of the brain involved in implicit memory: the basal ganglia and the cerebellum.

I won't go into brain physiology in any great detail here. Suffice to note that each of these different types of memory is supported functionally by different areas of the brain:

- Working memory - the prefrontal cortex
- Episodic memory - the hippocampus
- Implicit memory - the basal ganglia and cerebellum

Of these three types of memory, only implicit memory is impacted by memory reconsolidation. It would be more precise to label this phenomenon as Implicit Memory Reconsolidation.

The Role of Implicit Memory

Implicit memory affects the aspects of behaviour that occur without conscious awareness.

For instance, it involves our emotional responses. When you see an item on the news and you feel an automatic emotional response, these feelings come from implicit memory.

Implicit memory involves the autonomic nervous system. This is a crucial part of anyone's trauma response, so is extremely important.

Let me give an example. In the therapy room I used to work in, I noticed it became uncomfortably cold during the winter. So, I would approach the radiator on the wall to turn up the heating.

Often, when I touched the radiator control I would get a static shock that was not hugely painful, but was still unpleasant.

Eventually, I changed rooms. The radiator in my new room never gave a static shock. Yet every time I went to alter the controls, my body would react. I would feel a strong response physically. I felt nervous and would pause in response.

Every time I touched that control, I did so with trepidation.

My nervous system saw the similarity between this radiator and the one that had given me the shock. So, it responded every single time.

And that was just in response to a radiator!

The autonomic nervous system is deeply powerful and a big factor in why change is hard for our clients. As they are part of the implicit memory system, memory reconsolidation can erase and update these responses.

Think of a client with anxiety or panic attacks, or the shut down of depression. Think, too, of the many less obvious problems and blocks that are influenced by the response of the autonomic nervous system.

Hopefully, you can see the power of this approach to change the lives of your clients.

Implicit memory also includes conditioned associations. Imagine a client who says: "Whenever someone puts a hand on my shoulder, I feel sick because it reminds me of my abuser." They are referencing a conditioned association from their implicit memory system.

A more benign example of conditioned association might be how I often fancy an ice cream whenever I prepare to set off to the beach. For you, it might be a song that has you think of a particular vacation, or a smell that reminds you of a favourite place.

The Difference Between Story and Response

So, what happens once memory reconsolidation has occurred?

To explain this, we need to refer to two different types of memory - story memory and implicit memory.

Let's suppose that somebody has experienced a traumatic incident, perhaps an attack. Ever since the attack, they have had panic attacks and are chronically in fight or flight. These autonomic nervous system responses are triggered even without a present threat.

This happens whenever now resembles then, often in the most subtle of ways.

After memory reconsolidation, the client will still remember that the attack took place. After all, memory reconsolidation does not erase episodic memory. The client would be just as capable of describing the attack as before.

However, the distress responses from the nervous system would no longer occur. Memory reconsolidation will have changed the responses stored in implicit memory.

As such, the client will remember and be able to recount what happened, but without the charge and distress of the original memory.

As a result, this client would no longer be stuck in fight or flight and would no longer suffer panic attacks. These nervous system responses are overwritten in implicit memory with something more useful to the client. As such, it becomes easy for them to once again go out of the house and engage with life.

It is not *The Eternal Sunshine of the Spotless Mind.* The client retains their history and their story. But this trauma stops touching their life. Their nervous system responds to the present-day circumstances, not to those of the past.

Nervous System Level Change

There was a time when I used to run workshops in communication skills. These workshops covered techniques such as Nonviolent Communication, a helpful approach developed by therapist Marshall Rosenberg.

This technique promotes certain ways of communicating that result in choosing to share our feelings and needs rather than the other's wrongness.

For instance, instead of saying "You are lazy and disrespectful," we might say "When you don't arrive home at the time we agreed, I feel hurt because I need a connection with you."

This is a useful way of having difficult conversations, as it helps us avoid falling into a cycle of blame, defensiveness, and counter-attack.

There are many other similar strategies designed to help us communicate well in difficult moments.

But how easy are they to do when your nervous system spikes into high-level fight or flight?

As valuable as such strategies are, they fall down when humans move away from a feeling of safety. These systems are designed to help you escape life threats.

The nervous system is not designed to communicate openly with the sabre-toothed tiger. It is designed to spike the hell out of you so you get running fast - or at least put up enough of a fight that it finds a less bothersome prey.

Even someone with the best tools and strategies can find them too hard to access during a nervous system hijack.

This is the power of memory reconsolidation. Change happens in implicit memory, so it changes the things that happen on autopilot without our direct control.

The old nervous system responses do not occur. The client no longer blushes the way they always did. They no longer feel agitated. They no longer get dragged into the depression of shut down. Unless, of course, there really is a present danger.

The nervous system no longer reacts from a prediction error that what happened then is still happening now.

Instead, it is released to do the job it was intended for - to keep us safe in this moment based on an accurate assessment of whether we are in danger right now.

As a therapist, a key sign that memory reconsolidation has taken place is that change occurs at this fundamental level. Those things that we do not cognitively control now operate differently.

Change does not take willpower or determination. The involuntary responses simply no longer occur.

This is why it is easy for the client to maintain the change.

Summary

Let's have a quick recap of all the key concepts so far.

Memory reconsolidation is the only brain mechanism that produces lasting effortless change. This means that if such change has occurred, memory reconsolidation must have occurred also.

Memory reconsolidation is not a therapy model. Instead, it is a destination that your approach to therapy must arrive at. This means that you can largely continue with much of how you practice. Yet, you might tweak it so that you more reliably give the brain what it needs to trigger the mechanism.

When the result is permanent effortless change, memory reconsolidation explains this therapeutic success. As I mentioned before, if you can think of a client who got this kind of change from your work together, then you somehow triggered this brain mechanism.

Likewise, any therapy modality that can boast of such changes on a reliable basis must also be triggering memory reconsolidation.

When memory reconsolidation takes place, it literally erases old trauma responses. Because they are gone, it means relapse is impossible. Relapse occurs when people autopilot to those old brain pathways. By rewriting them, whenever they go there on autopilot, the brain finds new instructions.

As such, change takes place at a nervous system level and is effortless to maintain.

PART TWO

MAKING
TRANSFORMATIONAL CHANGE

CHAPTER 5

THE SEVEN STEPS OF TRANSFORMATIONAL CHANGE

In this section, I will show you the seven steps of transformational change. As well as discovering that memory reconsolidation exists, scientists showed us exactly what the brain needs to trigger it.

As therapists, this is useful as it allows us to translate those findings into our own practice - the very purpose of this book.

The seven steps of memory reconsolidation can be split into two sections: preparation and implementation.

There are three preparation steps, and three implementation steps, thereby completing the seven steps in total.

A quick pause is in order here. Perhaps you are feeling confused by the previous paragraph. Have you miscounted? Is there a typo? I clearly talk about seven steps, and yet three plus three is only six. What on earth is happening here?

My guess is that, if you noticed this anomaly, your brain became very interested in it. It's likely that you re-read the offending sentence to make sure you hadn't missed something.

This is what happens when a brain experiences anomalies. There is an increase in focus and it pays extra attention.

There is no typo. You have not missed anything. It was a cheap and deliberate trick played by me (sorry!) with a specific aim. At a microcosmic level, I wanted you to have a mismatch experience.

A mismatch experience is where an expectation is disconfirmed. You expected seven steps and I gave you six. Both statements could not be true. So, the brain pays attention.

The reason I wanted you to have that experience is because these mismatch experiences are key to the process of memory reconsolidation.

I will be talking more about the importance of mismatches and how to create them in the pages ahead. In the smallest way possible, you have hopefully now experienced an example of what I am referring to.

There Really Are Seven Steps

There are actually seven steps. I was leaving a step out on purpose. So, let's do it properly.

The credit for these seven steps goes to Bruce Ecker. He is a therapist and former scientist, and so is well equipped to dissect the scientific papers and make some sense of them for us.

From lab studies, Ecker has identified seven steps in three stages: prepare, implement, and verify.

He refers to this as ABC-123-V:

- ABC are the three steps of the preparation stage.
- 123 are the three steps of the implementation stage.
- V is where we verify that memory reconsolidation did take place.

In the pages ahead, I will break these down in some detail so that you can understand how to apply these steps to your own work.

Just Like Baking Cakes

The concept of prepare, implement, and verify is one that we experience in many other tasks too.

For instance, baking. If we decide to bake some cakes, we must first prepare. We get the sugar and the flour and any other ingredients. We prepare them so they are in a form that allows them to be baked. If we don't do this preparation stage, we can't end up with cakes.

Once the preparation stage is done, we can move on to the implementation stage. We get the unbaked cakes and put them in the oven.

Finally, the fun part. We verify that the baking process worked by tasting the cakes!

So it is with memory reconsolidation. We must first prepare. This process may look very similar to how you already work.

Once we have the information we need, we can then go ahead and try to trigger memory reconsolidation.

Finally, we check to see if it worked or not.

Preparation (ABC)

The preparation stage has three steps. You may notice that they are not too dissimilar from what you already do. This underlines my point earlier that you should be able to continue with the model you already favour, perhaps with a few tweaks.

The steps are:

A. Identify the problem.
B. Identify the target learning.
C. Generate some mismatch information.

Let's take each in turn.

A: Identify the Problem

This is the most straightforward step. After all, the client will typically tell you about the problem within the very first session.

I prefer to think of the problem more as the thing they want to change. It instantly gives the work a forward momentum. It lifts the client away from only being focused on the problem to thinking about what they would like instead.

Indeed, I tend to ask this kind of question. For instance: "So, suppose you were no longer anxious. How would you like to be instead?"

As well as shifting their focus a little, knowing what they want will also be therapeutically useful. It allows us to explore what happens in the body when they imagine themself getting it.

For instance, take the example of Vicki, who isolates herself from others. It is useful to know that what she really wants is to contact friends and make new acquaintances.

By asking her to imagine picking up the phone and contacting a friend, we give her an experience. In that experience, she connects to what happens in her body when she imagines doing so.

As trauma therapists, we know that trauma exists in the body. This is a result of the reaction of the autonomic nervous system. When we seek to make a change that the nervous system is not comfortable with, it will send messages of unease throughout the body.

Identifying these messages of unease will help you know how the nervous system responds. It is likely that this same response has occurred throughout life, and was learned during a moment (or a series of similar moments) that felt unsafe.

The client finds it easier to link to the trauma's origins when they connect to these specific sensations of unease.

It also offers the therapist a checklist of success. When Vicki attempts to call a friend and these responses are no longer present, change will be easy. At the end of the process, as we shall see later, these autonomic responses that were initially present will simply no longer be there.

The absence of these responses is a key indicator that memory reconsolidation has occurred. We cannot check for the absence of something without first knowing that it exists.

Investigating how life would be different once the client gets what they want is a key part of understanding the problem, and the body's protective fight against change.

As part of this investigation, it is helpful to make the problem (and thereby its solution) specific. This is why I always ask for concrete examples of how and where the problem shows up.

In the example given above, knowing that the client is isolated and wants to be connected to friends is not quite enough. More specificity is needed.

Therapist: So, tell me about a time recently that this problem showed up.

Vicki: On Friday I was so lonely. I ended up just going to bed early and sobbing.

Therapist: That sounds really tough. How would you have liked it to have been instead?

Vicki: I just wish I could have been around friends.

Therapist: So what happened that meant you weren't around friends? Were they already busy?

Vicki: I don't know. I didn't get in touch with anyone.

Therapist: Ok. So they may have been free, but you didn't reach out?

Vicki: Yes. I suppose they may have been.

Therapist: So, what's it like to imagine picking up the phone and giving someone a call to ask if they'd like to spend time with you?

Vicki: Ughh. No. I couldn't.

Therapist: What happens in your body when you think of doing that?

Vicki: I feel sick. My jaw tightens and my stomach flips.

Therapist: Keep checking your body. What else do you notice?

Vicki: I feel a tightness in my chest and everything goes tense.

Therapist: Ok, that makes sense. So your stomach flips, your jaw tightens, you feel sick and your chest feels tight and you notice a tension in your body generally?

Vicki: Yes, that's right.

This exchange helps us to understand what the problem is, when specifically it shows up, what they want to be doing instead, and what bodily responses are mobilised to oppose them doing it.

As you can see, this is a very rich description that goes beyond merely knowing that the client feels lonely and isolated.

B: The Target Learning

The concept of target learning needs a little more explanation. It is called target learning because, once removed, change will be easy for the client.

We can think of it as our target for removal. I sometimes describe it as the 'core prediction'. It represents a prediction of greater suffering should the client reach their desired goals, and so actively blocks them from doing so.

Think of the example of Vicki. We already know that her autonomic nervous system mobilises against her calling her friends. This is an embodiment of learning. Her nervous system, at some point, learned that this was the safest option.

If Vicki's nervous system updated that learning, calling a friend would no longer be so difficult. Indeed, it would feel easy and would happen naturally. The impulse to reach out to others would be unencumbered by a nervous system response that falsely predicted threat.

The same is true of other learnings, such as beliefs. Imagine if Vicki held a belief of: "Nobody truly cares about me, so what's the point in facing more rejection?"

No wonder it feels hard to ask a friend for company or support.

The core assumption when discovering target learning is to assume that the problem makes sense. No longer is the client assumed to be somehow disordered.

Instead, the belief or nervous system responses are rational, given their history. Indeed, it was an act of genius. The client figured out how to navigate these threats and pressures somehow - often when only a child.

Even if these approaches have now outlived their usefulness, they did work. The client is still here, after all. Whatever they went through, they survived. Their responses and conceptualisations were successful.

The target learning says that dropping this old strategy would make things even worse. They have a problem they want to change. Yet keeping that problem, at least as they currently see it, ensures that they fend off an even greater suffering.

After all, why aren't clients just changing without us? They know the problem. They know how they'd like it to be instead. We discover that early within the first session. Why isn't that enough?

Typically in life - and in the client's life too - when we want something we make it happen. The bin is full, we empty the bin. I want to sit in the sun, so I go into the garden. I feel dirty, so I get a shower.

Why is this particular change so difficult? Because the target learning means that the problem seems necessary to keep.

I often think of this as the monster in the corridor problem.

The Monster in the Corridor

Imagine a man - let's call him Simon. He spends all his time in a small, dark, dank room. It is cold in this room, yet he does not turn up the heating. He is not eating and he never leaves. It is an unpleasant place to be and he is miserable.

This might seem strange. It gets stranger still when we learn that, in the very next room, he has money stacked up in pile after pile. Simon is genuinely wealthy and it is his own money that he is fully entitled to spend.

Why then does Simon not just go next door, access his resources, and live a different life? Why does he live in cold, hunger, and darkness instead?

One may be tempted to find a disorder to label him with. But let us instead hold to the assumption that the problem makes sense.

As we investigate, we discover that in the corridor that separates these two rooms, there is a ferocious, bloodthirsty monster.

Simon's actions are no longer so strange. It makes sense that he won't leave his room and simply get his money. Moreover, all attempts to get him to leave his room are doomed to failure.

Change would be easy - if only there was no monster.

Once we show Simon the CCTV footage that proves that the monster has gone, Simon will leave his room and access his resources without any effort.

It is not the problem of not spending his money that needs to be tackled. Rather, it is the target learning that is the focus of change work.

Another way of thinking about this is the classic Mafia protection racket.

We see a shopkeeper regularly hand over $100 to someone who has done nothing to earn it. Why doesn't the shopkeeper simply keep that money?

Even though losing that $100 each week is a problem - it protects him from an even worse problem. It wouldn't be the best solution to help the shopkeeper say no to the gangster. The solution is to make the gangster go away. No gangster, no problem.

In the same way, our clients keep the problem even though they have had enough of it. It makes sense that they do, because it protects them from an even worse problem.

The target learning, whether it be a set of beliefs or autonomic nervous system responses, is what will be erased with memory reconsolidation. Once those beliefs and responses are gone, change becomes effortless.

During this step, we help the client to discover the underlying reason why having the problem still makes sense. It identifies the core learnings that we will seek to erase.

C: Mismatch

So far, we have looked at:

Step A: Identify the problem.

Step B: Identify the target learning.

In this final preparation step, we need to find some mismatch information. A mismatch is anything that disconfirms the target learning. The target learning represents a prediction that we want to update. As you will see later, mismatches create prediction errors which make the relevant brain pathway writable.

Let's take a simple example. You believe that all dogs are brown. I show you a white dog - a West Highland Terrier. Seeing a dog that is not brown gives you an experience that disconfirms your previous learning. As such, it is a mismatch.

It is important to be in touch with the target learning that reproduces the problem. When discovering mismatches, we need to find ones that disconfirm the target learning rather than something else.

Imagine a client who suffers with agoraphobia. If we have identified a target learning that expects ridicule if seen by others, showing this client a white dog does not help.

A white dog disconfirms his belief that all dogs are brown. But it does nothing to disconfirm his fear of ridicule.

Naturally, we cannot intentionally create a mismatch unless we have first identified a target.

How to Discover Mismatch Information

Therapists are already very good at digging for mismatch information and being alert to it.

For instance, exception questions are useful for finding mismatch information.

Let's take the case of Roger. He believes that he is not likeable. He tells himself a story that he is not worthy of friendship and cannot have friends because others do not like him.

Such stories are powerful. This story has a strong effect on Roger's behaviour and his experience of connection in life. He keeps away from people. He does not attend social functions. When others do engage him in conversation, he panics and ends the conversation as soon as he can.

An exception question inquires about when the opposite of this story is true. The therapist might ask: "Tell me about a time when you have had a friend?"

Similarly, Yvonne keeps missing opportunities in life. Others get promoted ahead of her even though Yvonne is more capable. She doesn't put herself forward for advancement.

When talking further, it becomes clear that she has a belief that bad things happen if you dare to go first.

The therapist might ask: "So tell me about a time when you did go first, and bad things didn't happen - or it maybe even worked out well?"

Exception questions invite the client to step outside of their story and find mismatch evidence from their own lives.

Sometimes exception questions can be about the lives of others too.

Philip believes that confident people are unpopular. He doesn't want to be unpopular. So, he discounts his own abilities and tells himself the story that he is worthless.

Again, we can ask about exceptions in his own life. "Tell me about a time when you felt confident and others approved of you and gave you positive attention."

We could also ask about the lives of others. "Who do you know in life who is both confident and well liked?"

Exception questions are also useful with the common belief of "I am stuck."

Think of Carla. She is in therapy and feels stuck in life. She says she is simply not capable of bringing the life she wants into being.

The therapist might help the client get specific about what that life looks like. A good question for this is the miracle question from Solution Focused Therapy.

Therapist: So, if a miracle happened overnight so that you woke up without the problem, what would you first notice that gave you a clue that this had happened?

Client: Oh, things would be so much calmer for a start. I'd wake up and the kids would be cooperating.

Therapist: What else would you notice?

Client: We'd actually have some time at breakfast. We'd chat with each other instead of being so rushed.

Therapist: Do you enjoy it when you all chat together at breakfast?

Client: Oh yes, it's so nice. It feels like we are a proper family.

Therapist: So it sounds like you've experienced that before to some extent?

Client: Yes, it was like that on Tuesday, actually. Everyone was calm. I'd got up a little bit earlier. It was only ten minutes, but it made all the difference. So at breakfast it just felt breezy.

This represents mismatch information. The initial belief of "I am stuck and I cannot bring the life I want into being" is disconfirmed by the knowledge that the change she wants is already starting to happen.

At other times, the role of the therapist is to catch mismatches that the client spontaneously brings into the conversation.

As clients talk about life, they inevitably share information that mismatches their target learning.

Think back to Roger, who believes he is not likeable enough for friendship. During a conversation he might say something like: "So I phoned my friend to see if he'd like to go for a walk."

Or he might say: "It's a shame I moved really. I loved living in that city. The people I worked with were really decent and welcoming. They just seemed to take me under their wing."

Our job as therapists is to be alert to these pieces of mismatch information that arise naturally in conversation. Clients will often share these mismatches without joining the dots.

As you will see later, part of our task in creating memory reconsolidation is to use this mismatch information to invite updated learnings.

CHAPTER 6

PUTTING IT ALL TOGETHER

You now understand the three preparation steps for memory reconsolidation work. You may notice that these steps are not too dissimilar from how you are currently working.

As I said earlier, memory reconsolidation work means you can tweak, rather than abandon, your preferred therapy approaches.

You have seen that the steps are:

Step A - Identify the problem.

Step B - Identify the target learning.

Step C - Identify mismatches to that target learning.

Let's put that together with a case example. This is the case of a young woman named Vicki, who we met earlier.

The Case of Vicki: Step A - The Problem

When checking for the problem, we need to:

- Hear what the client is telling us.
- Ask for a specific situation where the problem has shown up.
- Ask what they want instead.
- Check out their nervous system responses when they imagine getting it.

Vicki: I feel really down and isolated.

Therapist: That sounds hard. When does it show up for you?

Vicki: Oh, lots of times.

Therapist: Can you think of one in particular to help me better understand?

Vicki: It's like last week. I was going through a tough time with my boss and I felt really lonely.

Therapist: Yes, that's a good example. What would you have liked to have happened instead of feeling so lonely? What did you need in that moment?

Vicki: I would have really liked a friend to be there for me. Just to get stuff off my chest, you know?

Therapist: Absolutely. It really helps you to get stuff off your chest.

Vicki: Yeah.

Therapist: Do you have friends that you might have contacted?

Vicki: I do, but I don't tend to reach out when I'm like that.

Therapist: Okay, so supposing our work together changes things in the way you want. That might be a sign that things are better? That when you feel lonely or going through a tough time, you'd reach out and get the support you need?

Vicki: Yes, definitely.

Therapist: So take yourself back to that moment last week. And this time, just imagine reaching out to a friend. Think of someone in particular, and imagine reaching for the phone and calling. Imagine telling them that you're lonely and going through a tough time. Notice what comes up for you in the body as you imagine that.

Vicki: Ughh. It feels really uncomfortable. I feel really resistant to it.

Therapist: And that discomfort, if you didn't have a word for it, so you just had to describe what's happening in your body - what would you be describing?

Vicki: It's like my body is tensing and I notice myself pulling back. My heart speeds up too and I start to feel sick.

Therapist: Ah okay. So as you go to reach for the phone you notice that your body tenses and you start pulling back.

Vicki: Yes.

Therapist: And you feel sick and your heart goes faster.

Vicki: Yes, that's right.

Therapist: Tell me about the tension. Where does that show up?

Vicki: In my shoulders mainly.

Therapist: Right. Anywhere else.

Vicki: Yeah, my jaw. It goes tense in my jaw.

Therapist: So your shoulders go tense, and your jaw. Anywhere else?

Vicki: No that's it.

Therapist: And the sick feeling? Where is that? Is it your stomach? Your throat? Somewhere else?

Vicki: It's in the pit of my stomach.

Therapist: It sounds really uncomfortable.

Vicki: Yeah, it is. I just start to feel overwhelmed with it. I just want to get into bed and hide away.

In this exchange, the therapist has learned about:

- the problem.
- when it shows up.
- what the client wants instead.
- how their nervous system mobilises to stop them from getting it.

Vicki: Step B - Finding the Target Learning

As we have seen, the target learning is so called because when erased, the client will make the change they want with ease.

Vicki finds herself isolated, despite having a social network. In those moments when she most needs their support, she does not reach out to them and so robs herself of the benefits of such a network.

Our standpoint is that this makes sense. We just need to find out how and why.

This is not always easy work as the client may not be aware of the target learning themselves. Indeed, they may be mystified as to why this problem keeps showing up in life.

It is often a key moment for the client when, through this work, they gain an understanding of what is going on. A typical client response is to feel optimistic.

There are as many ways to discover the target learning as there are modalities. In the following pages of this book, I will outline three different ways to discover the target learning:

- The Single Sentence Formula
- External Personification of the Problem
- Child Obedience to Parental Injunctions

The Single Sentence Formula

One method I often use involves a repurposing of Motivational Interviewing questions. It helps lead to a single sentence description of what is going on for the client. That single sentence then reveals a core belief.

I call this approach The Single Sentence Formula.

The Single Sentence Formula repurposes and tweaks a sentence construction from therapist Niall Geoghegan. It follows this formula:

> **If I do the thing I want**
>
> **Then there'll be this terrible consequence**
>
> **So I carry on doing the thing I came here to change**
>
> **Even though I long to do the thing that I want**
>
> **Because ANYTHING is better than that terrible consequence.**

Note that this sentence construction needs just three pieces of information:

- What the client wants
- What the client fears
- The problem they are holding onto

Before looking at Vicki's case, let's use the earlier example of Simon and the monster in the corridor.

We already have the three key pieces of information needed:

- What Simon wants is to go next door and get his money.
- What he fears is that the monster will eat him.

- The problem he is holding onto is staying cold and hungry.

So let's see how that fits into the sentence:

If I go into the room next door and get my money

The monster in the corridor will eat me

So I carry on staying cold and hungry in this small, dank room

Even though I long to use my resources and look after myself

Because ANYTHING is better than being eaten by the monster.

Once this sentence is constructed, we see that Simon's behaviour is not crazy, but makes sense. It is self protective.

It also reveals the target learning. The target learning is the feared bad consequence. It is the outcome that ANYTHING (even the problem that they want to change) is better than.

For Simon, this was: "The monster in the corridor will eat me."

If it could be shown that there was no monster in the corridor, Simon would have no problem accessing his resources.

Similarly, if it could be demonstrated that the monster was a friendly vegetarian, Simon would again be happy to leave the room and access his resources.

When the client no longer needs the protection of the current problem, the change occurs naturally.

How to Find the Feared Consequence

To uncover the feared consequence in a real life case, like Vicki's, we can use Motivational Interviewing questions.

The standard four questions from MI are:

- How does the problem serve you in some way, i.e. what are the benefits?
- How does it cost you?
- How would the change cost you?
- What are the benefits of change?

This can be mapped on a quadrant like the one below:

BENEFITS OF STATUS QUO	COSTS OF STATUS QUO
COSTS OF CHANGE	BENEFITS OF CHANGE

The first question needs a gentle introduction. It can be a jarring question unless gently introduced in a way that acknowledges that.

Therapist: So this might seem a strange question, and I suppose it is in some ways because I know how upsetting it is for you to live with this problem. But in the way that many bad situations will sometimes bring some positives too, I'm wondering what positives this problem brings, even amongst all of its bad aspects. What are the ways that it serves you to not reach out when you need support?

Vicki: Well, I don't want to be THAT person!

Therapist: Which person is that?

Vicki: Oh you know, the burden. My friends have their own problems too.

Therapist (writing it down on the quadrant): Okay, so it stops you from feeling like a burden.

Vicki: Yes, definitely.

Therapist: How else does it bring a benefit or serve you somehow?

We stay with this question, asking what else and recapping the list, until the client is out of benefits.

Notice how, at this stage, the client's answers are not questioned but simply acknowledged and collected. In Vicki's case, the quadrant containing the benefits looks like this:

BENEFITS OF STATUS QUO	COSTS OF STATUS QUO
Stops me being a burden My stuff stays private Hard to be gossiped about Nobody cares about me anyhow so what's the point Saves me from rejection Easier to not reach out than get tumbleweed More independent Gives me space to be more reflective Sometimes get the answer myself	
COSTS OF CHANGE	BENEFITS OF CHANGE

The next question is: How does it cost you?

The answers to this question don't help us find the target learning, so I won't spend time exploring this here. Yet the chance to reflect on how the current problem gets in the way can be motivating. Most importantly, it does give the client's brain something different to think about - especially as the next question is similar to the first.

The third question looks at the costs of change. It is a good idea to acknowledge the similarity of this question to the first question.

Therapist: So, staying with costs, let's look at the costs of change. It's a similar question to the first one, but from a different angle. There might be some overlap, but asking this way can often bring up a few answers you hadn't thought of last time. I'm interested in what the costs of changing are. So, imagine if you became that person who reached for your phone each time you needed your friends. What price would you pay for being that person?

Clients will often make the point that it would be good to have the change. Agree that it would be good. If they give reasons why it would be good, I'll put their answers in the final quadrant.

For example:

Vicki: Well, it would be good rather than bad. I'd actually have some support.

Therapist (writing the word Support into the final quadrant): Yes, that makes sense. You'd have support, and no doubt a range of other good things too. I'll ask about those good things in a moment. But for now, see if you can get in touch with anything that would be a bad outcome of being this way.

This part works best when we make the process experiential rather than cognitive.

Therapist: So maybe close your eyes for a moment, and really connect to that version of yourself who simply reaches out to your friends when you need to. You're that person now. When you need support, you just ask for it. You don't even question it. That's who you are now. Really get into that and feel that. (Pause). What comes up for you that feels uncomfortable about the fact that this is who you are now? What price might you pay for being her? What are the possible costs of making this change for you?

In Vicki's case, it looks like this:

> People would get sick of me
>
> No one cares about me anyhow
>
> I'd face a lot of rejection
>
> I'd get too dependent on others fixing things for me
>
> I'd hate when they snub me while I'm already down
>
> I can't face even more upset when already struggling

Vicki's quadrant may now look like this:

BENEFITS OF STATUS QUO	COSTS OF STATUS QUO
Stops me being a burden My stuff stays private Hard to be gossiped about Nobody cares about me anyhow so what's the point Saves me from rejection Easier to not reach out than get no response More independent Gives me space to be more reflective Sometimes get the answer myself	Isolated Lonely Unsupported Miss out on being with friends Get stuck in my own head Tend to get depressed Problems seem overwhelming Tired of doing everything alone
COSTS OF CHANGE	BENEFITS OF CHANGE
People would get sick of me No one cares about me anyhow I'd face a lot of rejection I'd get too dependent on others fixing things for me I'd hate when they snub me while I'm already down I can't face even more upset when already struggling	

The final question is about the benefits of change. Again, this doesn't help us with finding the target learning, but can be motivating for the client.

The left side of the quadrant reveals what the client sees as a benefit of keeping things as they are, and downsides of making the change they want. Together, they are listed below:

Stops me being a burden

My stuff stays private

Hard to be gossiped about

Nobody cares about me anyhow so what's the point

Saves me from rejection

Easier to not reach out than get no response

More independent

Gives me space to be more reflective

Sometimes get the answer myself

People would get sick of me

No one cares about me anyhow

I'd face a lot of rejection

I'd get too dependent on others fixing things for me

I'd hate when they snub me while I'm already down

I can't face even more upset when already struggling

Finding The Emotional Weight

The next step is to ask the client which of these has the most emotional weight. For instance, the sense of not being gossiped about wasn't a huge concern for her. It came out as she brainstormed, but lacked emotional weight.

When asked which items seemed the most emotionally heavy, she chose the fear of reaching out and everyone proving that nobody cares about her.

Her answer reveals the bad consequence, and the underlying belief.

We now have the three data points we need:

- What she wants
- What she fears
- The problem she is holding onto

Using these three pieces of information, we construct the sentence together like so:

If I reach out to my friends when I am feeling down

They won't respond, and will prove that nobody truly cares about me

So I keep myself isolated in times of trouble

Even though I long to reach out and get support from my friends

Because ANYTHING is better than experiencing not being cared about.

We can see how Vicki's isolation makes sense, despite her large social network. If she believes that nobody truly cares for her, why would she reach out and suffer feeling unimportant to those closest to her?

Notice how this identifies the target learning.

Imagine if Vicki had learned in life that the people around her care for her and want to offer support. It would then be easy to reach out.

But life has given Vicki a different learning that robs her of the ongoing support that is now readily available.

Together, we have discovered that the target learning is: nobody truly cares for me. Once this belief is updated, the change that she wants will be easy.

There are, of course, other ways to discover the target learning. I will describe some alternative approaches from various modalities in the coming pages.

External Personification of the Problem

There is a useful technique within Narrative Therapy that invites the client to turn the problem into an external persona.

For instance, Larry suffers with anxiety. He is invited to create an external persona of the anxiety. It is now not something within him, but something external to him. Some clients like to think of it as a kind of gremlin.

In this way of thinking, it is the gremlin that produces the anxiety. Larry no longer must defeat himself, but overcome the gremlin. Self destruction is no longer implicit in the therapy.

It promotes a way of Larry improving his meta-cognition skills. When he feels anxious, he can notice that the gremlin must be present doing its thing.

In this work, the therapist and the client join forces like investigative journalists doing a feature about the gremlin. It is an approach that creates a stance of curiosity.

Our job is to learn as much as possible about the gremlin. Ultimately, we want to find out why the gremlin is so keen on intervening in Larry's life to give him feelings of anxiety.

Almost always, the client will reach an understanding that the gremlin is like an over-zealous friend seeking to protect them. This kind of exploration is aimed at seeking to discover how and why.

Below, the therapist uses this technique to explore the tactics of the gremlin and help the client discover the anxiety's purpose.

Therapist: What is the gremlin's favourite technique for giving you anxious feelings?

Larry: Well, there are a few I think.

Therapist: Does one come to mind?

Larry: If I'm around people, it tells me that everyone wishes I would go away.

Therapist: Oh wow, well, that would certainly do it. What happens when it tells you that?

Larry: Well, I start thinking that I'm not likeable.

Therapist: Right. So it drops in the thought that everyone wants you to go away. And then it drops in another thought that you're not likeable.

(Notice the subtle readjustment that it was the gremlin that dropped in the thought rather than the client thinking it. This aids the separation.)

Larry: That's right. I start to feel all panicky.

Therapist: I see. So, what feelings does it have you feel when it wants to make you anxious?

Larry: Well, my heart starts to go faster and I feel my face burning up. And my stomach is all jangly. And my hands start to get all clammy.

Therapist: I see. So, it notices you doing fine with these people. So it jumps in and tells you that, actually, everyone wishes you'd go away. And then it tells you that you're not likeable. Then to top it off, it puts all those feelings in your body.

Larry: Yeah. It jumps in whenever I'm doing ok with people. It's like it wants to mess it up or something.

Therapist: Why does it do that, do you think?

Larry: I don't know. Maybe it hates me or something. It wants me to have a shit life and be lonely.

Therapist: I guess it must feel like that, huh? You're doing fine and then it sees that and messes it up.

Larry: Right. It's a real pain.

Therapist: Totally. I see that. So, when the gremlin sees you doing fine with other people and it decides that it needs to intervene, what's going on for the gremlin? What emotion is it feeling?

Larry: Erm. I don't know really. It's hard to say.

Therapist: If you think of some of the key emotions - is it feeling happy to see you doing so well?

Larry: Ha, no. It's not happy.

Therapist: Is it scared, or sad, or angry?

Larry: No, not angry as such. It's kind of panicky itself.

Therapist: Oh really?

Larry: Yeah, it's anxious. It kind of jumps in all worried.

Therapist: That's interesting. So it seems to be worried for you?

Larry: Yeah, I guess it is. It's all jangly at me doing well with people. Like it's trying to protect me somehow.

Therapist: Ah, okay. So it seems kind of protective?

Larry: I'd not thought about it like that before, but yes. It's kind of like when I see my daughter reach for something that might hurt her and I dash in.

Therapist: Ah, I see. So it's got the same fear and anxiety that you feel when you see that your daughter is on the verge of hurting herself.

Larry: Yes.

Therapist: So, this is interesting. You're saying that the gremlin is trying to help you and keep you safe, just as you do with your daughter?

Larry: Yes.

Therapist: What do you think it is trying to keep you safe from? Why does it get so scared when you get on well with people?

Larry: I'm not sure.

Therapist: Sit with it a second. Be with the gremlin and get curious about it. Why does this creature, who is trying to protect you, think it's not safe for you to be doing well with people?

Larry: It doesn't want me to get hurt.

Therapist: Emotionally hurt or physically?

Larry: It doesn't want people to get too close to me.

Therapist: I see. Where did it learn that people getting close to you can hurt you?

Larry: It doesn't want me to lose myself like I did with Mum. It's like I didn't exist in my own right. She was so controlling and suffocating.

Therapist: I see. So when the gremlin sees you doing things that might bring people close to you, it tries to protect you from that control and suffocation?

Larry: Yes. It doesn't want that. It doesn't want me to get hurt and lose myself.

Therapist: Right. So it messes it up for you by making you think they don't want you there.

Larry (chuckles): It does, yes.

We can clearly see the target learning from this exchange. By allowing Larry to get curious about this external persona, he learned that it had a protective function.

He was able to identify that the gremlin was fearful of his smooth interactions with potential friends. As he investigated some more, he noticed that the gremlin had a fear that Larry would lose his agency and identity to overpowering others.

The gremlin had decided that anything was better than that.

Even though we did not use the Motivational Interviewing approach to reach the target learning, we can still write it as a single sentence using the same format as before:

> **If I allow myself to think well of myself when with others**
>
> **Then they'll get too close and overpower me**
>
> **So I tell myself that they don't like me and become anxious**
>
> **Even though I long to have fun and easy conversations**
>
> **Because ANYTHING is better than being overpowered and losing myself and my agency.**

Likewise, in Vicki's case, these same kind of questions would discover her gremlin's protective function. Vicki's gremlin works hard to stop her reaching out to friends. It does this because it doesn't want her to experience the pain of disregard. Most of all, it wants to spare her the suffering of others not caring about her.

Child Obedience to Parental Injunctions

Bob and Mary Goulding were psychotherapists who blended aspects of Transactional Analysis and Gestalt Therapy to create Redecision Therapy.

Transactional Analysis has a concept called script decisions. The founder of Transactional Analysis, Eric Berne, believed that we make life decisions as children. We then live them out faithfully, much as an actor with a script.

Childhood decisions are made in order to help the child survive, navigate, or explain their circumstances.

The Gouldings, in an attempt to codify these script decisions, developed a list of twelve injunctions. An injunction is a perceived invitation or command from the parent. It may not have been the parental wish or intention. It represents the child's sense of what would be better to avoid.

As with any injunction, each of the twelve Goulding injunctions begins with the word "Don't".

Inviting a client to ponder and select which injunctions apply to them can offer a shortcut to the target learning.

The injunctions are:

- Don't be / don't exist.
- Don't do anything.
- Don't be a child.
- Don't grow up.
- Don't be you.
- Don't make it.
- Don't feel.
- Don't think.

- Don't belong.
- Don't be close.
- Don't be important.
- Don't be well / sane.

In some ways, to think of these as parental injunctions is less helpful than simply viewing them as childhood decisions.

For instance, in the last chapter we met Larry and explored his anxiety gremlin. The gremlin would get agitated if he did things that might lead people to get close to him.

Had Larry looked through these injunctions and noticed which felt true for him, it is likely that he would have selected Don't Be Close.

We saw how Larry was faithfully obeying that decision. As a child, he had made the decision that "Yikes, I'd best not get close to anyone else if this is what it's like."

Notice that Larry's mother seemed to be commanding the very opposite. It is the decision that little Larry made in response that is important.

Now, when he goes against that script decision, he reminds himself of the expected danger that comes with it.

A client will often notice that more than one injunction applies. Larry, who was not allowed to make his own choices, might have made other decisions such as Don't Think, or even Don't Be Important.

To look at another case, Jeanette is considered by others to be a serious and formal person. She does not join in when others joke around in the office. She judges them negatively and focuses only on work.

She spends hours in the office and is there most nights long after others have gone home. Then she takes work home with her for the weekend.

When she does attend recreational events, she notices herself feeling stiff and awkward. Even when she pushes herself to join in, she finds it hard to let herself go. She tends to not participate and, at times, even feels resentful of friends who are more playful.

When a friend's child had a birthday party, most of the adults jumped on the bouncy castle while the children were being entertained. Jeanette did not and noticed that she felt cross at those who were having so much fun.

When she looked through the injunctions to see if any of them resonated, she immediately picked out Don't Be A Child.

When the therapist explored how she made that decision, she described a stiff and formal household where noise and play was discouraged. Her parents were neither neglectful nor abusive. But the environment felt overly mannered, and any exuberance was frowned upon.

She loved her parents and didn't want them to disapprove of her. She figured out that the best way to keep their love was to edit out her own playfulness.

Although using a different modality, we can nonetheless get to the Single Sentence formulation:

> **If I allow myself to be playful and to have fun**
>
> **Then I'll be judged as silly and irresponsible**
>
> **So I focus on work and censor my playful instincts**
>
> **Even though I long to join in and let myself go and enjoy life**
>
> **Because ANYTHING is better than Mum and Dad being disappointed in me.**

We have the target learning - that being playful and having fun means she will be judged negatively as silly and irresponsible.

Returning to Vicki's case, she might identify the injunctions of Don't Be Important and Don't Be Close. Her experience growing up is that when she sought closeness, it was spurned. When she brought her own needs, they were usually overridden by the needs of others. She decided that she was not important enough, and so took on both injunction decisions.

Vicki: Mismatch Information

We have already seen that, when talking with clients, we must either discover mismatch experiences or be alert to them when they arise.

In Vicki's case, as often happens, some mismatch information was shared when recounting her week.

Vicki: It's been a stressful week.

Therapist: Really? What's been happening for you?

Vicki: Well, I'm okay. But I had to go to the hospital late on Thursday night.

Therapist: Are you okay?

Vicki: Yes, it turned out to be nothing in the end, so I'm fine. But it was pretty scary at the time.

Therapist: Yes, it sounds scary.

Vicki: I was short of breath and I got really worried about it and in the end decided to go to Accident & Emergency.

Therapist: Good for you for looking after yourself.

Vicki: Yeah. But you know what the wait is like there. I was there for literally six and a half hours.

Therapist: Wow, that's a long wait, especially if you're feeling worried for your health.

Vicki: I know. I was there until about five in the morning.

Therapist: How did you get through such a long, scary wait?

Vicki: Well, Jenny was there.

Therapist: Your friend?

Vicki: Yes.

Therapist: Okay, so she came with you to the hospital?

Vicki: Yes, she was at my place at the time. We had been watching a movie when the problem started.

Therapist: And so she went with you.

Vicki: I told her not to. I said just go home, I'll be fine. But she wouldn't. So she came with me.

Therapist: And it helped that she was there?

Vicki: Yes, it did. She took my mind off it. It was really good of her because she stayed the whole time.

Therapist: So she stayed with you the whole time?

Vicki: Yes. I kept telling her to go, but she wouldn't.

Therapist: That's a long time to stick around.

Vicki: I know, right? It was six and a half hours until I was seen.

Notice how the therapist hasn't generated this mismatch through exception questions. The anecdote itself has raised the mismatch. Yet the therapist is alert to potential mismatches of her target learning.

In this instance, the therapist has logged that there is a mismatch experience that can be used.

The target learning is: Nobody truly cares for me, so what's the point.

The mismatch is: My friend Jenny stayed all night with me at A&E.

We know that this is a mismatch because Jenny staying so long with Vicki disconfirms the idea that nobody truly cares for her. Likewise, Vicki makes several invites to Jenny to go home and get some rest. Each time, Jenny refuses, acting out of care for Vicki.

Both statements cannot be true. If nobody truly cared for Vicki, Jenny would not have stayed all night in order to care for her.

Note also that the therapist has not uncovered information that was new to Vicki.

The target learning has already been discovered at this point. Jenny's presence at A&E is also no revelation. Vicki is already aware that the person with her at A&E was Jenny.

Mismatch work is typically not a moment of new discoveries. Rather, the client is aware of the information, but hasn't joined the dots. They don't yet notice that this experience potentially disconfirms the core belief.

Preparation Summary

Let's recap. We have seen that memory reconsolidation work, like baking, requires some preparation.

The preparation stage consists of the following steps:

    A. Identify the problem.

    B. Identify the target learning.

    C. Identify the mismatch information.

When identifying the problem, we need to pay attention to:

- What the client wants to change.
- A concrete example of when and where it shows up.
- What they want instead.
- The autonomic nervous system responses when they try to get what they want instead.

The target learning explains how the problem makes sense for the client. In other words, the problem is not just a problem. It is also a defence against or a solution to another bigger problem. Once that perceived bigger problem is erased, change becomes easy.

Mismatch information is anything that disconfirms the target learning. This can be discovered through exception questions, or by being alert to the client's spontaneous sharing of mismatch information in their life.

In Vicki's case, her problem was one of isolation when she most needs support, and the loneliness that comes with it.

The target learning is that she believes that nobody truly cares for her, so what is the point. Not reaching out for support protects her against the bigger problem of the pain of disregard.

The mismatch information we have discovered so far is that her friend Jenny spent six and a half hours with Vicki at the hospital, even when she had permission to leave Vicki alone.

In the next chapter, we will discover how to put this information together in order to invite memory reconsolidation.

CHAPTER 7

TRIGGERING TRANSFORMATIONAL CHANGE

Before we get to the steps needed to trigger memory reconsolidation, I want to first talk about magic.

There is a parallel between what skilled magicians do and what memory reconsolidation therapists do.

Magic tricks have three distinct phases. First, the magician builds an expectation. Next, there is a bridge event. Finally, there is a moment of surprise.

As an example, think of the rabbit in the hat trick. It's so well known now that there is no surprise anymore. But imagine that you have never seen a magic trick before, and let's follow the steps.

The magician builds an expectation in the audience by placing a live rabbit in a top hat. This builds the expectation that, all things being equal, that is where the rabbit shall remain.

Next, there is a bridge event, where the magician waves a magic wand and yells abracadabra.

Finally, the magician shows the inside of the top hat and - surprise - the rabbit has disappeared.

All magic tricks involve these steps. They all rely upon an expectation being overturned. The magician invites the audience to make a prediction, and then surprises the audience by creating a prediction error.

It is not only magic that works this way. Jokes do too. The comedian misleads the audience into one expectation, and then upends the expectation in the final line of the joke. This moment of surprise creates laughter.

The Scottish comedian Frankie Boyle once described his job as "writing sentences that have surprising endings."

For example, here's a joke from comedian Gary Delaney:

"I've never been very good with faces, which is why I'm no longer a plastic surgeon."

The opening of the sentence creates an expectation that he means this phrase in the usual way - that he can't remember faces. The ending of the sentence upends that expectation, creating the surprise and the laugh.

Magic and comedy are based on the surprise of prediction errors. So, too, is memory reconsolidation.

The Predictive Brain

In order to appreciate the importance of surprise, it is worth understanding something about the brain first.

We often experience the brain as a reactive thing that responds to external stimuli. After all, we see a tasty cake, and in response we begin to salivate.

As such, we assume that the brain is reacting. Yet that is only a fraction of the story and overlooks the brain's real job - to make predictions.

When the brain receives external stimuli, it moves into immediate prediction mode. It asks: "Given these external stimuli, what is my prediction about what this human needs next?"

When we see the cake, we do not salivate in response to the cake. We salivate in response to the brain's prediction that those juices are needed to eat the cake.

If the brain was simply reactive, we would have a lot of problems. For example, every time we stood up, we would faint. The brain constantly predicts what we need next and makes changes in the body to ensure that we are prepared for it.

When I move from a seated to a standing position, my brain recognises the initial movements and muscle tensions, so predicts I am about to stand. Because of that prediction, it makes bodily changes so I am prepared by the time I am standing. Hence, no fainting.

Only prediction can achieve this.

When your nervous system moves into fight or flight, it is because the brain predicts that you may need to fight or flee. Think of a leisurely evening walk in your neighbourhood. You turn the corner and there's a gang. You notice yourself moving into a higher state of alert, maybe even feeling a bit anxious.

Your brain is seeing the external stimuli of the gang, recognises that the situation is not as safe as it was a moment ago, and so predicts that you may need to move soon.

The increased heart rate and feeling of adrenaline is your brain's predictive role in action. It is ensuring that your body is ready to move if it needs to.

When the external stimuli are more subtle and less easily identified, it might be called anxiety. Yet the same process is occurring. The brain is making a prediction - perhaps an outdated one - that your body may need to fight or escape. It is seeing signs of an unsafe situation and preparing you physiologically for what it believes you may need to do.

In trauma, when something now resembles then - even if subtle - the brain takes that data and predicts the best way to maintain safety. Depending on the person's history, it may predict that they need to escape. Alternatively, it may predict that there is no solving this problem and that shutting down is the best course of action.

Either way, the autonomic nervous system is responding to a prediction of what the body needs in order to best keep that person safe. These predictions were likely accurate back when they were first formed.

Take the client who is constantly on alert as an adult and can never relax. As a child, they grew up in a household that was violent and volatile. It makes sense for that child to be constantly on alert. Relaxing in a volatile home could prove dangerous. Far safer to be always monitoring the mood music for signs of the next outbreak.

Now grown, they are not facing that same danger. Yet the brain still bases its predictions on that old data. The nervous system is activated into chronic anxiety even when danger is not objectively present.

The meanings that we make of traumatic learning become predictions too, in the form of beliefs. See how Vicki had a belief that nobody truly cared for her. This belief was actually a prediction.

It took the form: "If I reach out for help when I'm struggling, nobody is going to care anyhow, just like nobody cared back then."

As we shall see next, the key to updating that prediction is to generate prediction error. Prediction error, like the magic trick, generates surprise and invites the brain to update its learning.

The Magic of Memory Reconsolidation

We saw how the magician uses a three-step process to generate the surprise of prediction error:

1. Invite the audience to make a prediction

2. Abracadabra

3. Produce a prediction error

The same occurs when doing memory reconsolidation work. Just like a magician, the goal is to give the client an experience of the prediction being broken.

The magician has to create the prediction by clearly showing that there is a rabbit in the hat.

In therapy, the expectation or prediction has already been generated by the client's life experience.

They arrive with these predictions already formed. When Vicki believes that nobody truly cares for her, this is the lens she sees the world through. It feels true to her, and so she makes predictions about the behaviour of others.

These predictions impact how she behaves as a result. Friends who would prefer to give care are denied the opportunity because Vicki predicts otherwise. Like the man with the monster in the corridor, Vicki's resources are available yet not accessed, limiting her enjoyment of life.

For a magician, the bridge experience is the waving of the magic wand, which leads to the surprise of a rabbit-less hat.

For therapists, the bridge event is the client having a mismatch experience that generates the same level of surprise. Surprise is the end result of a prediction error. In Vicki's case, she predicts a lack of care, so is surprised when she realises how the presence of care disconfirms that.

The Role of Surprise

Speaking of tricks, do you remember I played one on you earlier? I said there were seven steps to memory reconsolidation, then listed only six. I did this to deliberately give you an anomaly experience.

Anomaly experiences are key to memory reconsolidation because they generate surprise. Not just any surprise, but a surprise caused by prediction error.

When predictions are broken, the double take effect does something important in the brain itself. It opens that brain pathway for rewriting.

We saw earlier that neuroscience has demonstrated that the brain can change trauma response. Brain pathways work like combination safes - both protected and yet also able to open and have the contents changed.

The surprise of a prediction error is the combination (or code) that unlocks the safe. When a mismatch lands with the client, the door of the safe swings open. The brain pathway becomes changeable where previously it was locked.

Now that we understand the key importance of surprise, let us dig into the implementation stage of memory reconsolidation.

Implementation - Easy as 1,2,3

Ecker stated that the seven steps of memory reconsolidation are summed up as ABC-123-V.

ABC are the preparation steps of find the problem, find the target, find the mismatch.

The implementation steps are:

1. Reactivate the target learning
2. Activate the mismatch
3. Repeat

But what does that mean in practice?

Let me simplify it for you. The three steps are like a game of conkers.

If you're not familiar with the game of conkers, let me quickly explain. A conker is the heavy brown seed of the horse chestnut tree. It has a hard, glossy shell.

A favourite childhood game of mine was to collect these conkers when they fell to the ground in autumn. Then we would tie one to a shoelace and do battle against the conkers of our friends.

Each child takes turns at hitting their rival's conker. Time and again, the conkers are brought together.

For memory reconsolidation, one conker is the target learning, and the other is the mismatch experience. Like any good conker contest, these two are brought together repeatedly.

Let's use Vicki's example again. Her target learning is the belief / prediction that nobody truly cares for her. The mismatch information is that her friend stayed with her at the hospital in order to care for her.

The game of conkers means that these must be brought together repeatedly for memory reconsolidation to occur. The first goal is to generate surprise. This unlocks the brain pathway. Once the mismatch has landed and the pathway is writable, our job is to keep bringing these 'conkers' together.

It is this repetition that rewrites and updates the brain pathway for good.

Mismatch experiences can occur in a number of ways.

They can be imaginal. We will look at imaginal versions in the final part of the book.

They can be conversational. This involves bringing two pieces of knowledge together so as to join the dots.

Next, we will see an example of conversational mismatching.

A Conversational Example

In the transcript below, we will see Vicki talking with her therapist. Notice in this exchange that the therapist does the following:

- Spots the mismatch
- Tightens the mismatch
- Brings both pieces together
- Repeats

I'll include the earlier conversation and add to it with the new.

Vicki: It's been a stressful week.

Therapist: Really? What's been happening for you?

Vicki: Well, I'm okay. But I had to go to the hospital late on Thursday night.

Therapist: Are you okay?

Vicki: Yes, it turned out to be nothing in the end, so I'm fine. But it was pretty scary at the time.

Therapist: Yes, it sounds scary.

Vicki: I was short of breath and I got really worried about it and in the end decided to go to Accident & Emergency.

Therapist: Good for you for looking after yourself.

Vicki: Yeah. But you know what the wait is like there. I was there for literally six and a half hours.

Therapist: Wow, that's a long wait, especially if you're feeling worried for your health.

Vicki: I know. I was there until about five in the morning.

Therapist: How did you get through such a long, scary wait?

Vicki: Well, Jenny was there.

Therapist: Your friend?

Vicki: Yes.

Therapist: Okay, so she came with you to the hospital? (Spots the mismatch)

Vicki: Yes, she was at my place at the time. We had been watching a movie when the problem started.

Therapist: And so she went with you.

Vicki: I told her not to. I said just go home, I'll be fine. But she wouldn't. So, she came with me.

Therapist: And it helped that she was there?

Vicki: Yes, it did. She took my mind off it. It was really good of her because she stayed the whole time.

Therapist: Wow, so she stayed with you the whole time?

Vicki: Yes. I kept telling her to go, but she wouldn't.

Therapist: That's a long time to stick around.

Vicki: I know right. It was six and a half hours until I was seen.

Therapist: So how come she stayed with you through the night? Does she enjoy being in A&E? (Sharpens the mismatch)

Vicki: No. Who does? She was there to look after me and make sure I was ok.

Therapist: Right, I understand. So she stayed all those hours in order to look after you. She wanted to know you were ok.

Vicki: Yes. She's a good friend.

Therapist: So I'm curious, how is that for you? To feel, on the one hand, that nobody cares for you. And at the same time experience your friend staying at the hospital for no other reason than to care for you? (Brings both pieces together)

Vicki (stares silently)

There is a long moment of silence here.

Vicki: I don't know really. It's strange.

Therapist: Right. So when you think of that old belief that nobody truly cares for you, and then you think of Jenny being there because she cares for you, it feels strange. (Repeats bringing the pieces together so both are held in mind simultaneously.)

Vicki: Yeah. It's confusing. I don't know. It's confusing.

Therapist: I get that. I can see how it's confusing. There's this old belief that nobody cares for you. And then there's Jenny staying up the whole night in order to care for you. That's a confusing combination, I can see that. So, what comes up for you as you hold that confusion? (Repeats holding both)

Vicki (laughs): I dunno. I guess they both can't be true.

Therapist: Yeah, I suppose not. So it's either one or the other?

Vicki: Well, it's confusing to me.

Therapist: Yeah.

Vicki: But either nobody cares for me or Jenny does, I suppose.

Therapist: Yes, I suppose that's right. Your sense is that these two things clash.

Vicki: Yes. Well they do, don't they?

Therapist: So what's that like for you? To notice that the old belief that nobody cares for you clashes with the fact that Jenny really does. (Repeats)

Vicki: I guess it feels weird. Like it doesn't feel as strong.

Therapist: So the old belief feels looser now?

Vicki: Looser, yes, that's it.

Therapist: So go back to that old belief for a moment and connect to that.

Vicki: Yes.

Therapist: And then put yourself back in the hospital with Jenny by your side, refusing to leave even when you give her permission. What's that like? (Repeats)

Vicki (after a pause while she revisits the scene): Well, it makes no sense.

Therapist: It makes no sense?

Vicki: Yes. Obviously, she cares for me.

In this conversation, the therapist noticed the mismatch and then started the game of conkers. The target learning was the old belief that nobody cares. The mismatch experience was the time at the hospital with her friend Jenny.

The therapist invited the client to hold both thoughts in her mind at the same time. Previously, each aspect of knowledge existed separately. By bringing the two together, the hope was that a mismatch would be experienced by the client.

Notice that the therapist did not declare the mismatch, but simply invited the client to experience it.

Mismatch attempts don't always land. Yet there is a clear sign from the client that this mismatch did. It seemed to generate a response of surprise.

Such surprise can be expressed in different ways, but this time it was a focused silence. The therapist did not disrupt the silence. This was valuable 'penny drop' time.

The therapist then continued to invite the client to hold this mismatch. As the juxtaposition became more untenable to the client, the old belief began to loosen.

Finally, the therapist asked the client to revisit the old belief one more time and then experientially return to the hospital with Jenny by her side. The client, almost derisively, rejects the old belief.

How to Know If a Mismatch Lands

Our aim is to give the clients a mismatch experience that lands with them. The reason we do this is because this moment of mismatch makes the brain pathway rewritable. It unlocks the door of the combination safe.

How do we know that a mismatch experience has landed?

There are a number of ways that a client can show this. It typically manifests as a moment of surprise.

You will have seen this look before.

Think of any prank-based TV show you may have seen, like the old 1970s show Candid Camera. A person is placed in a situation that they think is real. But in fact, everyone is an actor playing a part.

For instance, perhaps a team of builders turns up to start work on something in the person's garden. He knows nothing about this and doesn't want this building in his garden. But they say it's sanctioned by the government to hold waste sewage. "You'll have had a letter," they say.

The homeowner isn't best pleased, saying he's never had any letter and they're not building in his garden.

The scene plays out for a while. The homeowner becomes increasingly immersed in the situation until there is a reveal when the host appears. We see a moment of confusion. The penny drops and the new reality is understood.

That "penny drop" moment is what we are looking for. It is a look of realisation as one reality competes with or gives way to another.

It can be a look of focus as the brain pays attention to the new information of the mismatch.

The brain's default mode is the efficiency of autopilot. Once it knows something, it doesn't keep figuring it out anew. It becomes the accepted and unquestioned reality.

When a mismatch lands, the brain focuses. It recognises that this is potential new learning that needs attention.

The brain will focus on novelty once it is aware of it. Noticing novelty is, after all, a safety issue for a prey animal like us. An anomaly in one's construction of reality is essential to pay attention to.

As in Vicki's case, there is often a moment of silence as the client becomes lost in thought.

At other times, the client's focus is not so still. There is a look of confusion or realisation, and the eyes dart about as they seek to come to terms with the mismatch.

In this moment, I never ask the client how they make sense of it. I don't want them to square this circle.

Such a question removes them from the experiential mismatch and instead invites the logical brain to re-establish its original way of seeing the world.

Let the client have this experience of mismatch. It is a profound one. The brain may try to justify it anyhow. Its barrister needs no invite from us.

Another way that mismatches can land is through laughter. Surprise can often induce laughter. As we saw earlier, the job of a professional comedian is to write surprising endings to sentences. With comedy, we are tricked into one idea of the world and then reality is revealed.

In the same way, it is not unusual for mismatches to have a comic element that results in laughter from the client.

Next, you will encounter a case where the mismatch landed with a roar of laughter.

The Weeping Boxer

Kyle is a young man in his early thirties. He suffers with rages that he wants to control. During therapy, it becomes apparent that Kyle never cries. Yet he often feels emotions that lead him to fight back his tears.

In those moments, Kyle produces rage instead. In our work together, we realise that his rage is a cover for the emotion that he really feels, which is sadness.

We explore how it might make sense that he does not allow himself tears, even when he feels like he desperately wants to cry.

Kyle explains that he believes that men who cry are not real men. He picked up this message from his immediate family of origin with the common mantra of "boys don't cry".

This was reinforced culturally by growing up watching gangster movies. He decided that to cry would renounce his manliness.

He didn't want his rage either, but it was better than not being respected as a man. Better to be rageful than be seen as weak or contemptible.

His rage worsened in the aftermath of a key bereavement. He noticed that he did not cry even at the funeral. As before, he masked it with rage that was threatening his key relationships and leaving him isolated at the very time he most needed support.

With the target learning revealed, we needed to find or create a mismatch.

As often happens, Kyle provided one himself in the description of the funeral scene. In passing, he mentioned a cousin who is a professional champion boxer. This cousin fitted Kyle's framework of what it meant to be a man.

Yet Kyle mentioned how his cousin openly sobbed at the funeral. This was a great mismatch opportunity.

Therapist: So, imagine how that would be, to walk up to your cousin at the funeral as he openly sobs and tell him, "Look at you crying, you're not a real man."

Kyle: (laughs out loud) He'd probably give me a smack!

In this moment, the mismatch had landed. Kyle's old belief was challenged once he held it alongside this other piece of information. He could update and widen his conception of what it means to be a man, and what is allowed for a man.

Given such a clear sign that the mismatch had been experienced, I chose to stay with this juxtaposition, exploring it further in order to repeat it. My hope was that, in the repetition, memory reconsolidation would be triggered.

Next time I saw Kyle, he had visited the cemetery and wept openly in front of others.

CHAPTER 8

HOW NOT TO MISS MEMORY RECONSOLIDATION

You may notice that a lot of what has been explained so far sounds similar to what you already do in your work. This is true. I did promise that you wouldn't need to abandon your ways of working - only to tweak them. Hopefully, you can see that too.

However, we do need to make sure that we are practicing in such a way that erasure takes place.

Earlier, we saw how competitive therapy sought to build new brain patterns to compete with the trauma brain pathways. We saw its usefulness, yet we saw how it made relapse possible.

Erasure therapy is different because it overwrites the trauma response, meaning it can not return. Change is permanent. It requires no effort from the client in order to maintain it.

As practitioners, we need to get skilled at recognising when we are merely building competitive pathways.

We need to understand what happens in the brain itself during therapy and what the brain needs in order to trigger memory reconsolidation.

When a mismatch lands, the brain pathway that we want to change becomes rewritable. It stays that way for four to five hours. It is useful knowing how long this window lasts. It means that you do not need to panic if the client goes off on a tangent. You can relax and know that the brain pathway remains rewritable at least for the length of your session and for some hours afterward.

However, a rewritable brain pathway in itself is of no value, unless we rewrite it. Think again of the analogy of a combination safe. The mismatch unlocks and opens the safe. But the contents stay the same unless we replace it with something else.

If all we do is open the safe, then nothing changes. Four to five hours later, the safe will automatically lock itself again. The outcome? Nothing. Things are as they were before.

Likewise, if all we do is make the brain pathway rewritable for a few hours, the client will not benefit.

In order to rewrite the pathway, the brain needs the mismatch to be repeated.

Three Ways to Miss Memory Reconsolidation

Even though a lot of the descriptions so far may look like what you already do, it is easy to miss memory reconsolidation, even when transformational change is within your grasp.

Many journeys look the same, but have a different destination.

My neighbour and I can make the exact same trip. We can sit on the same train, in the same carriage. We can walk the same route from the station to our street. Yet ultimately, we end up in different houses.

Likewise, don't assume that just because your work looks similar that you are triggering memory reconsolidation. Don't toss this book aside thinking that this is something you clearly already do. You may not be.

The key is not in the nature of the journey, but whether you do the key steps of mismatch and repetition. Indeed, even therapists who use the same modality can differ in this regard.

When comparing notes, two therapists will agree that they are doing the same thing. But the crucial difference is in the existence of a mismatch experience that is repeated.

In Vicki's case, memory reconsolidation was triggered after we learned that her friend Jenny showed extraordinary care for her. Together, we used that information as a potential mismatch experience.

Thankfully, it landed with Vicki so we held the mismatch in order to repeat it. This resulted in memory reconsolidation and the change that comes with it.

But we could easily have had the same ingredients and missed it. Here are three ways that would have failed to give the brain what it needed.

Example 1: No Mismatch

Vicki: It's been a stressful week.

Therapist: Really? What's been happening for you?

Vicki: Well, I'm okay. But I had to go to the hospital late on Thursday night.

Therapist: Are you okay?

Vicki: Yes, it turned out to be nothing in the end, so I'm fine. But it was pretty scary at the time.

Therapist: Yes, it sounds scary.

Vicki: I was short of breath and I got really worried about it and in the end decided to go to Accident & Emergency.

Therapist: Good for you for looking after yourself.

Vicki: Yeah. But you know what the wait is like there. I was there for literally six and a half hours.

Therapist: Wow, that's a long wait, especially if you're feeling worried for your health.

Vicki: I know. I was there until about five in the morning.

Therapist: How did you get through such a long, scary wait?

Vicki: Well, Jenny was there.

Therapist: Your friend?

Vicki: Yes.

Therapist: Okay, so she came with you to the hospital? (Spots the mismatch)

Vicki: Yes, she was at my place at the time. We had been watching a movie when the problem started.

Therapist: And so she went with you.

Vicki: I told her not to. I said just go home, I'll be fine. But she wouldn't. So she came with me.

Therapist: And it helped that she was there?

Vicki: Yes, it did. She took my mind off it. It was really good of her because she stayed the whole time.

Therapist: Wow, so she stayed with you the whole time?

Vicki: Yes. I kept telling her to go, but she wouldn't.

Therapist: That's a long time to stick around.

Vicki: I know, right? It was six and a half hours until I was seen.

(In the previous example, the therapist spots the mismatch and invites the client to hold it. In this example, it happens differently.)

Therapist: You have a good friend there.

Vicki: I really do.

Therapist: And her being there took your mind off things?

Vicki: Yes, it really helped.

Therapist: What difference did it make for you?

Vicki: I was calmer. More relaxed. I wasn't going into catastrophe mode like I would have done. And I was less bored. It was still a long wait, but she definitely made it easier.

Notice that the therapist is only discussing the effect of Jenny's care. It reinforces the benefit of having support from friendships. But no mismatch is invited. At no point is the therapist sharpening the mismatch information, or joining it with the old belief so the two can be held together simultaneously.

Given there is no mismatch, the brain pathway remains locked. No memory reconsolidation will occur here, even though it was possible.

Example 2: No Repeat

Another way to miss memory reconsolidation is to create the mismatch experience, then move on. Let's imagine a client, Jeff, who has a belief that if he openly shares his hobbies and interests with others, he will be ridiculed.

Jeff: I went to a house party on Saturday.

Therapist: Okay, how did it go?

Jeff: Well, these things aren't really my thing, so I left pretty frustrated.

Therapist: What was the frustration?

Jeff: It's always the same with me. Someone approaches me and I clam up again.

Therapist: Did that happen this time?

Jeff: Yeah, a guy called Warren started chatting with me. He seemed ok and things were going well enough. Then he asked me what kind of things I'm into in my spare time. And I froze.

Therapist: And if you'd allowed yourself to share your interests, what do you fear would have happened?

Jeff: Well, if he knew the kinds of things I like doing, he'd have laughed at me and maybe told other people at the party. Then everyone would be laughing at me and making fun of me, and I'd hate that.

Therapist: That's a scary thought.

Jeff: Yeah.

Therapist: If you'd have answered Warren honestly, what would you have said?

Jeff: Well, I like playing Scrabble. I love it actually. And I'm really into fantasy books. But I couldn't have said that. Everyone would just laugh at me and make fun.

Therapist: Tell me about a time where you *did* share your interests with someone and it went well for you.

Jeff: (thinks) Well, maybe the time I told Tom.

Therapist: Your friend Tom?

Jeff: Yes. But I didn't know him that well then. I remember we were talking and I mentioned I'd been to the bookshop, so he asked me what I like to read. I froze for a moment but for some reason I told him the name of the book I'd bought.

Therapist: Yeah? What did he do?

Jeff: He got really interested. He'd read the book the previous month and it turns out we are both big fans of that author.

Therapist: A fantasy author?

Jeff: Yeah. Tom and I have read everything he's ever written.

Therapist: So, what's that like, Jeff? First of all, to really feel the truth of that old story. The one that showed up at the house party that says "If I share my interests they will laugh at me and mock me." To really feel the truth of that prediction in your body.

And while feeling that, step into that other experience with Tom, where sharing your interests got such a positive response. That you actually bonded over it and became firm friends because of it.

What is that like for you to believe, on the one hand, that sharing will bring ridicule, and yet at the same time to notice that in this real life experience with Tom, sharing brought bonding and friendship?

Jeff: (Stares into space for many seconds as it lands)

Jeff: It's pretty weird. It's confusing really.

Therapist: Yeah, it must be. So how did you feel after the party?

Jeff: Frustrated really. I just wish I could enjoy those things more.

Therapist: How did you soothe the frustration in the end?

Jeff: I beat myself up for a bit about what a loser I am, I ate some crisps, and then got tired and ended up falling asleep.

Notice how the therapist asked a question to bring about a possible mismatch: "Tell me about a time where you did share your interests with someone and it went well for you."

Notice that, on this occasion, it did result in some mismatch information.

Notice that the therapist then attempts to generate a mismatch experience. The therapist invites Jeff to hold both of these truths at the same time.

Jeff does, and we can see evidence that it has landed with Jeff. This light bulb moment is an external sign that the mismatch has opened the brain pathway. It is now possible to rewrite this old response and change Jeff's story.

Memory reconsolidation is simply waiting to occur. It needs the therapist to stay with the mismatch, gently repeating it in order to give the brain what it needs to complete the rewrite.

Instead, the therapist misses the repetition and moves on. A moment for permanent change is missed. If the therapist had understood the steps needed to trigger memory reconsolidation, they would have known to keep repeating the mismatch.

Sadly, for both Jeff and the therapist, the discussion moves on and the opportunity is missed. Eventually, Jeff becomes frustrated by a lack of progress and leaves therapy. The therapist feels frustrated too that their best efforts did not result in the change that was hoped for.

Example 3: Challenges Not Experiences

Let's look at another common way that memory reconsolidation opportunities can be missed.

When therapists first learn about the mismatch nature of memory reconsolidation, it is common for them to think that the key is to "challenge" clients.

They mistake mismatch for challenge. As a result, they believe that their role is to debate their clients into acceptance of the falseness of their beliefs.

The therapist then notices that these mismatches are not helping much. They do not lead to the miraculous changes that I share in this book. The therapist decides that it is all bunkum and so reverts back to old ways of working.

Yet, a challenge is not a mismatch. A mismatch is experiential. It is not a case to be made by the therapist. It is something that, in Bruce Ecker's lovely phrase, the client "bumps into".

Take the example of Vicki and her experience with her friend Jenny. Jenny had stayed six and a half hours with Vicki waiting in the emergency room overnight.

Here's how the original therapist helped create a mismatch experience.

Therapist: That's a long time to stick around.

Vicki: I know, right? It was six and a half hours until I was seen.

Therapist: So how come she stayed with you through the night? Does she enjoy being in A&E?

Vicki: No. Who does? She was there to look after me and make sure I was ok.

Therapist: Right, I understand. So, she stayed all those hours in order to look after you. She wanted to know you were ok.

Vicki: Yes. She's a good friend.

Therapist: So, I'm curious. How is that for you? To feel, on the one hand, that nobody cares for you. And at the same time, experience your friend staying at the hospital for no other reason than to care for you?

Vicki (stares silently)

There is a long moment of silence here.

Vicki: I don't know, really. It's strange.

Notice how the therapist takes no side here. They simply bring the two truths together and invite the client to experience holding both. As a result, the client independently experiences mismatch.

Contrast this with another therapist who mistakes mismatch as meaning challenge.

Therapist: That's a long time to stick around.

Vicki: I know, right? It was six and a half hours until I was seen.

Therapist: So how come she stayed with you through the night? Does she enjoy being in A&E?

Vicki: No. Who does? She was there to look after me and make sure I was ok.

Therapist: Right, I understand. So, she stayed all those hours in order to look after you. She wanted to know you were ok.

Vicki: Yes. She's a good friend.

Therapist: So your belief can't be true, can it?

Vicki: How do you mean?

Therapist: Let me explain. Jenny staying with you at A&E disproves the idea that nobody cares for you. People do care for you. Jenny cares for you.

Vicki: I suppose.

Notice that, in this case, the therapist has given a lecture instead of an experience. The client responds, but in a way that indicates compliance rather than mismatch.

Nothing has landed here for the client. A mismatch opportunity was available. Sadly, the therapist missed it by taking sides in the debate between the old truth and the new mismatching evidence.

As there is no mismatch, so there is no possibility here for memory reconsolidation.

The brain pathway remains closed. The chance of transformation is squandered.

Summary

Let's recap what we have covered in this section.

Bruce Ecker outlined the steps of memory reconsolidation work (ABC-123-V).

They are split into three stages:

- Prepare (ABC)
- Implement (123)
- Verify (V)

In the preparation stage, the task of the therapist is to identify:

A. The problem.

B. The core learning that keeps the problem alive (known as the target learning).

C. Some mismatch information that disconfirms it.

In the implementation stage, the task of the therapist is to play conkers with the client. We do this by offering an experience where the old truth and the mismatching information are explicitly brought together.

The steps are:

1. Activate the target learning.
2. Activate the mismatch.
3. Repeatedly bring together the target learning and the mismatch.

Anatomically, the key points to remember are:

- When the mismatch lands, the brain pathway opens.
- The repetition of the mismatch rewrites the brain pathway.

A mismatch alone makes no change. It is the repetition that erases the old trauma responses.

We will look at the verification stage (V) later in the book. Verification is where we check to see if our attempts to trigger memory reconsolidation have been successful.

So far, we have looked at conversational ways to introduce mismatch experiences.

In the next section, we will look at how to create mismatch information by using imaginal scenes. We will then see how to verify that change has taken place.

PART THREE

IMAGINAL TRANSFORMATION

CHAPTER 9

CREATING IMAGINAL MISMATCHES

The use of the imagination has an established history within therapy. In the earlier example of 'The Weeping Boxer', Kyle was invited to step into an imagined scene.

This was not done in any set-piece way. Instead, as part of a conversation, he was called upon to imagine something.

Therapist: So, imagine how that would be, to walk up to your cousin at the funeral as he openly sobs, and tell him, "Look at you crying, you're not a real man."

These conversational calls on the imagination happen commonly in therapy conversations, and many others.

Whenever we ask a question such as "What would that be like?" we are calling the client into their imagination.

In a more structured way, there are techniques like chair work that are used in Gestalt Therapy and Redecision Therapy.

Such approaches explicitly call upon the imagination of the client to communicate with people not actually in the room.

Earlier, we saw a technique within Narrative Therapy that invites the client to imagine that their problem is personified externally.

The client imagines a relationship with, say, the Anxiety Gremlin.

They continue to use their imagination to think about the gremlin's tactics and intentions, and other useful information.

Even the Miracle Question in Solution Focused Brief Therapy is a call upon the imagination of the client.

These calls upon our clients' imaginations are a key tool of therapy. Indeed, Human Givens therapists are taught that imagination is one of our innate human resources.

The use of imagination also has an evidence base to support its effectiveness.

Let's look at just three examples:

- The Ideal Parent Figure Protocol
- Goran Hogberg's Four Way Processing Protocol
- The Rewind Technique

The Ideal Parent Figure Protocol

In their book *Attachment Disturbances in Adults*, Daniel P. Brown and David S. Elliott outline a treatment path for working with trauma. This involves three key pillars:

- The Ideal Parent Figure Protocol

- Metacognitive interventions

- Fostering collaborative capacity and behaviour

The first of these pillars, the Ideal Parent Figure Protocol, uses the imagination as a source of self parenting.

This protocol invites the client to imagine that they were raised in a different family from their family of origin. It asks them to imagine that their parents from this family were ideally suited to their nature.

From that premise, the client is then asked to use their imagination to experience a range of scenes. In these scenes, these ideal parent figures provide: safety, attunement, reassurance, expressions of delight, and unconditional support.

In my own practice, I use an amended version of this protocol, tweaked so as to meet the requirements of memory reconsolidation.

When I use this approach with clients, it produces powerful experiences. When combined with the distress of their trauma, it will often invoke the mismatch and repeat necessary for trauma removal to take place.

A study by Parra, George, Kalalou and Januel (2017) investigated the effectiveness of this imaginal approach. Clients suffering with severe CPTSD were offered four sessions of therapy.

During these sessions, they experienced an Ideal Parent Figure visualisation lasting sixteen minutes. Each was also given a recording of the visualisation script to repeat at home.

They found that there was "a significant decrease in symptoms scores and increase in quality of life scores...with medium to large effect sizes."

Although the Ideal Parent Figure protocol was designed as a longer term treatment, in this short time, 20% of participants became securely attached.

These changes occurred even though the sessions were solely imaginal. Moreover, eight months later, the results had held.

Goran Hogberg's Four Way Processing

Goran Hogberg is a Swedish psychiatrist. He conducted a study into the use of imaginal reenactment with depressed and suicidal youth.

His protocol uses imaginal resources throughout. The imagination is used to:

- Create a place of safety.
- Revisit a distressing scene from the past week, seeing the event as remembered.
- Inhabit the scene directly to activate nervous system responses in the body.
- Remake the scene so that any suppressed movements or other impulses are now acted upon.
- Embody an animal that expresses those same movements.

- Positively reimagine the scene how they wish it had been.
- Imagine a future scene where the same situation goes well.
- Return to the place of safety.

As you can see, the imagination is doing a lot of work here.

Sometimes it is used to revisit the past. At other times, to reimagine the scene how it was wished to have been. Later, to imagine becoming an empowering animal. Then, to imagine a future where it all goes well.

To bookend all of this, imagination is used to both create and return to a place of safety.

Using this protocol, the study treated fourteen suicidal adolescents. Each was described as suffering post-traumatic symptoms and disturbed mood regulation.

Thirteen of the fourteen had lost their severe symptoms within four to twenty sessions. These changes were still in place when the adolescents were followed up with twenty-two months later.

That the positive changes were still present nearly two years later is a sign that memory reconsolidation has occurred. Remember that memory reconsolidation erases trauma. As such, the changes are permanent and effortless to maintain.

Hogberg's study is an example of this kind of transformational change.

The Rewind Technique

The Rewind Technique is an approach to working with trauma, especially individual traumas such as a road traffic accident.

The result is that clients who suffered anxiety, intrusive thoughts, and flashbacks no longer do. They stop needing to manage their symptoms as they no longer have symptoms to manage.

The technique itself has a number of variations. It has its roots in Neuro-Linguistic Programming (NLP) where it was then known as the Visual Kinaesthetic Dissociation Technique.

Dr David Muss teaches a version of it. He wrote about it in the British Journal of Clinical Psychology in 1991. In this study, he used the Rewind Technique to treat nineteen police officers who suffered from PTSD. The officers were followed for two years. It was successful for all officers and, crucially, none suffered a relapse.

Human Givens therapists also use a modified version of the Rewind Technique to treat PTSD and phobias.

The steps of the Rewind Technique are:

- Visualise a safe place before the incident.
- Watch yourself watching a TV screening of the traumatic event.
- Enter the movie briefly and rewind quickly to the safe place.

The client is invited to fully relax. They are then invited to watch themselves watching a TV that shows the trauma event. The aim here is to help create distance between the client and the trauma.

It is easier to watch a film of oneself experiencing a traumatic event than to directly experience it. It helps the client not be overwhelmed. Watching oneself watch the film adds a double dissociation that makes it easier to tolerate.

The film begins before anything bad happens. So, for instance, if there was a road traffic accident, it would begin with the client safely and happily in the car.

The film then shows the traumatic incident as it happened.

Once complete, the client imagines floating into the TV scene so they are in their own body, viewing things in the first person, inside the movie.

They are now in the movie, seeing things through their own eyes.

They are then asked to experience the scene being rewound at speed. They experience moving swiftly backwards in time through the traumatic event until they reach the safe beginning of the film.

This happens quickly, like rewinding a film with a remote control. They will visualise objects in the scene move away from them as they are pulled back through the rewind. For instance, if another car hit them in the original scene, they will see that car moving further away as the scene is rewound.

The film ends when they are back at the safe starting place at the beginning of the movie.

This process is repeated until the client no longer feels any emotion or response.

Notice how this approach is entirely dependent on the resource of the imagination.

Shona Adams and Steve Allan's 2018 study into the Muss version of the Rewind Technique found an 87% success rate. Their other study in 2019 into the Human Givens version found that 91% of clients were either recovered or reliably improved.

Working Directly with Implicit Memory

As you can see from these three example methodologies, the use of the imagination is a powerful tool for therapeutic transformation. Not only does it have an established history in therapeutic work, but a strong evidence base too.

It makes sense that it is effective, as the imagination works directly with implicit memory. Remember that implicit memory is the aspect of memory that is overwritten when memory reconsolidation is triggered.

In many ways, imagination is the perfect interface to the implicit memories we wish to access and change.

Implicit memory focuses on feelings. It stores our emotional responses, and the autonomic nervous system responses that show up in our bodies.

Remember that memory reconsolidation does not eradicate the story memory. Clients will still know what happened. It is the implicit memory that is reconsolidated. Despite being able to recall what happened, the emotional and nervous system response will be different.

For instance, imagine a client, Brian, who had been violently assaulted by an adult neighbour when he was nine years old. Once memory reconsolidation has been successfully triggered, he will still know that this attack took place. He will be able to tell the story of what happened just as before. Yet the distress it usually triggers will now be gone.

Given that our aim is to work with the implicit memory system, we can use the feelings from this system as a source of mismatch.

In earlier examples, we saw how the therapist might use exception questions in order to tease out evidential mismatches. The client's lifelong beliefs then get the chance to bump into some contradictory evidence.

The client who believes nobody cares for her bumps against the realisation that her friend cares for her so much that she stayed at the hospital with her. This new evidence is a source of mismatch.

As the client seeks to hold both truths in mind at the same time, reconsolidation may occur.

Yet a mismatch can also occur between the feelings generated in the original scene, and mismatching feelings generated by experiencing a new scene.

There are just two ways to have a new experience. One is to have the experience in life itself. This is not always possible, and even where it is, it can take a while to occur.

A more reliable way to have an experience is to imagine it.

When we use our imagination, we inevitably trigger the kind of emotional or nervous system responses that are stored in implicit memory.

Imagination can have us feel emotions like sadness, excitement, or fear. It can speed up the heart rate and dilate the pupils.

It may seem strange that the imagination has such power. But think of when you are reading a thriller. The squiggles on the page provoke your imagination. As your imagination constructs the scene, your nervous system and emotional responses kick in.

You are on the edge of your seat, eyes wide, urging the hero to escape the jeopardy. You feel disappointment and sadness when a much-loved character in the book dies, even though they are purely fictional.

In the same way, we use the imagination to time travel forward to places of dread or excitement. The holiday we are looking forward to brings feelings of joy and happiness.

A forthcoming meeting with an awful boss brings us feelings of dread. Neither event is happening in this moment, but accessing the imagination creates emotional responses and activates the nervous system.

Likewise, at some point, we have all woken from a nightmare with the heart pounding and coated in sweat. The nervous system is in full fight-or-flight mode, triggered by nothing but the imagination.

The imagination gives us access to emotions and nervous system responses.

By using the imagination, we can conjure feelings and nervous system responses that mismatch the expectations of the implicit memory.

The implicit memory predicts that one set of feelings will emerge from a given scene, yet experiences the opposite feelings instead.

With conversation, a lot of time can be spent trying to discover mismatch information. With imaginal work, we can simply create it.

The Power of the Nervous System

The young woman stood thirty-five feet high on top of the platform. It had taken her a while to clamber up each of the many ladders.

Her intention was clear. She would dive into the swimming pool below from the highest platform. The climb itself took a lot of effort. But she did it anyhow. She was determined.

Yet now, as she looks over the edge, a scared and strangled noise escapes from her throat. Involuntarily, her legs walk her three steps backward.

She had decided to jump. Yet her autonomic nervous system is not in agreement. It applies a force to move her away from the edge.

She fights it, of course. She steps forward once more. She looks down at the pool below. She braces herself to jump. Yet she does not.

Again, she is moved backward. She doubles over as if winded. Her anxiety is clear.

She gathers herself for another try. She walks quickly with purpose to the edge, more determined than ever.

Yet again, this internal force will not permit her. She reaches the edge and stops still.

This scene is taken from the 2016 short documentary film *Ten Meter Tower*. This movie simply shows the attempts of people to leap off a ten-meter platform into a swimming pool below.

Each person has chosen to. Their nervous system makes a different decision. The movie portrays this internal tug of war.

It demonstrates the power of the nervous system to stop us from doing things we say we want to do.

It is a good metaphor for the struggle we all face in life whenever change is hard.

When clients tell us the changes they desire, they tell the truth. But if their system believes the change is a threat, this powerful involuntary force will fight against them.

When working from a memory reconsolidation perspective, it is our job to discover the predictions that stop the client from getting what they want. When these blocks are removed, change is easy and mundane.

I am thirsty. So I get a glass of water. I am hungry. So I make a sandwich. I want to be able to read at night time. So I switch on the light.

All change is easy unless it isn't. When it isn't, the block is often a prediction that fears some kind of threat.

For these aspiring divers, the nervous system sees the height of the diving board as a threat. Even though there is a swimming pool below, it is a long way down. The nervous system intervenes in service of their safety and survival.

When clients find change hard, similar things are occurring.

Memory reconsolidation requires the discovery of such target learnings. Once erased, it becomes easy for the client to get what they want.

The responses of the nervous system, the emotions we experience, and the bodily sensations that show up for us are all examples of target learning.

The power of these feelings and responses can act as an urgent STOP sign when we seek to make the change that we most want.

Likewise, when the nervous system notices that the current situation resembles unsafe moments from our history, it intervenes. It plays out the responses and feelings we experienced then. After all, they were successful. They got us through threat and danger so that we survived. Why wouldn't the brain replay this tried and tested response?

This is why people suddenly feel anxiety as if from nowhere, or a panic attack out of the blue. The sophisticated nervous system notices that something in the now resembles back then. The old responses kick in.

When we seek to do something that wasn't safe for us back then, we are like the divers frozen on the diving board. We long to do it, but the nervous system stands in our way. It believes that this new behaviour is still a threat today. So naturally, it prevents it.

Think of the man who complies with everyone because as a child he dared not defy his father. The woman who still people pleases, and subjugates her own needs as a desperate attempt to win scarce love. The worker who wants a promotion but never applies for the job - because it's safer to be invisible.

When they seek to break this old programming, they become the divers on the diving board. Their nervous system, in a zealous attempt to protect them, stands in the way of the very change they want.

These feelings - the nervous system responses, emotions, and bodily sensations - are the target learnings to be erased.

The nervous system's responses are vital for our safety and survival, of course. But when its predictions are so outdated as to no longer be useful, they can be changed.

Creating Mismatch

These feelings are the target. Without these outdated feelings, the change would be easy. The mismatch will be the opposite feelings that meet their needs.

The old programming says, "When now resembles then, have these scared feelings and responses." After memory reconsolidation, the new programming will be: "When now resembles then, have these neutral calm feelings instead."

If a client felt scared, we mismatch with feelings of safety. If they felt ignored, we mismatch with feeling heard and validated. If their body froze in terror, we mismatch by generating action.

The benefit of working imaginally is that we can simply create these mismatches. We can use imagination to generate the new, positive feelings.

There are, perhaps, an infinite number of ways to do this. For instance, many therapies already use the concept of creating a "calm scene". The Ideal Parent Figure Protocol creates imaginal ideal parent figures to meet the client's relational needs.

I incorporate many of these approaches into my own practice. Yet, one approach that is consistently reliable in my work is imaginal reenactment.

Imaginal reenactment finds a scene that represents the old learning. For instance, it may be a traumatic scene from childhood. We then go through a specific protocol to imaginally reenact that scene in the client's favour.

Imagination creates feelings. By using the imagination to give the client what they need, the new feelings generate mismatches.

The client experiences something that, at first, looks like a bad scene, but instead provides the client with exactly what they need. The system expects this trigger to produce distressing feelings. Instead, it produces positive feelings.

We need not wait for mismatches. We can actively create them.

CHAPTER 10

A ROAD MAP
FOR IMAGINAL WORK

As we have already seen, there are many ways to do imaginal work so that memory reconsolidation can occur. The Ideal Parent Figure Protocol, Goran Hogberg's Four Way Processing, and the Rewind Technique are just a few of them.

In this section, I will talk you through an approach that I developed to trigger memory reconsolidation.

It is the imaginal technique that I use most with my clients. This is a protocol for imaginally reenacting painful events so that they are reimagined in the client's favour.

Finding A Scene: The Movie Question

In order to reimagine a scene, we first have to identify one that feels relevant to the client. So, how can we do that?

To help with this, I created a technique that I refer to as The Movie Question. With this method, I help clients find a scene to work with. The Movie Question supposes that the client's current struggle is a movie and they are the hero of it. Naturally, the director of the movie wants to show the audience how the hero got to this point.

Let's say that the hero believes nobody truly cares about them. The audience will want the movie to show a few scenes that reveal how they came to believe that.

Almost all movies show these origin stories. Think of Batman. Why does it make sense that Bruce Wayne, a wealthy businessman, is a vigilante crime fighter by night?

In the movie *Batman* (1989), we see the young Bruce Wayne emerging from the cinema with his parents. We see them walk along a darkened street together, still smiling and sharing popcorn. Suddenly two muggers emerge. A struggle ensues and both of his parents are murdered in front of him.

Now we get it! No wonder he isn't just enjoying his millions. No wonder he feels compelled to spend his nights on the streets fighting crime as Batman. It all makes sense.

The Movie Question asks: In the movie of your life, what are the scenes we could show the audience that would help to explain your current struggle?

Often, the client will identify more than one scene. It is a good idea to ask for scenes (plural) rather than to ask for a single scene. This subtly invites the client to come up with more than one, which adds to their sense of choice and control over the process.

Learning Why the Problem Makes Sense

We saw earlier that our focus as therapists is not the problem itself. Instead, we seek to discover why it is so essential to keep hold of the problem.

For instance, when working with a client who is tormented by guilt, we may be tempted to focus on the guilt. Instead, we must discover their "monster in the corridor". We want to learn why it is so emotionally necessary to keep hold of the guilty feelings.

Likewise, we saw earlier how Vicki felt isolated and alone. Our discovery work revealed that she does not reach out to friends when she is struggling. We learned that this is because she believes that nobody truly cares for her.

Her single sentence identifying this was:

> **If I reach out to my friends when I am feeling down**
>
> **They won't respond because nobody truly cares about me**
>
> **So I keep myself isolated in times of trouble**
>
> **Even though I long to reach out and get support from my friends**
>
> **Because ANYTHING is better than experiencing not being cared about.**

So, with Vicki, we are not asking for a movie scene that shows an explanation of her aloneness. Rather, we want to find scenes that explain how she learned the belief that nobody truly cares about her.

For Bruce Wayne, perhaps his statement might be:

> **If I allow myself to enjoy my evenings**
>
> **I will lose the people I most care about**
>
> **So I spend my life carrying the weight of the world on my shoulders**
>
> **Even though I long to enjoy life**
>
> **Because ANYTHING is better than losing those I most love.**

With Bruce Wayne, we are not asking for a movie scene that explains why he fights crime every night - although that may sometimes get us there too.

Rather, we are asking for a scene that tells us how he learned that enjoying himself results in losing the people he loves most.

This gives us richer detail. Now Bruce tells us how he connects the murder of his family to the enjoyable evening they'd spent. He is able to describe this scene in terms that are more psychologically connecting.

This scene is no longer just the event of the traumatic murder. It is the moment he learned his psychological stance that says: enjoying oneself is something we pay for.

It makes sense that he won't allow himself to enjoy life even though he wants to. A part of himself forbids it - and it makes sense why.

We can sometimes follow a client's nervous system responses as an opening for the movie question. A client who is anxious experiences feelings that suggest a lack of safety. We can ask the movie question to connect with that nervous system response.

Therapist: What scenes might the director include that would show how your nervous system learned this response?

The Movie Question is useful because it provides some distance for the client. They are able to separate their movie character version of self from their actual self. This separation allows clients to reflect more easily.

In my experience, clients like this idea of their struggle being the story of a movie. They understand how, in movies, the hero's struggle must make sense - and that we get to discover how.

This all helps to re-establish the basic stance of our work - you are not crazy, this makes sense somehow - so let's find out how.

As such, clients come up with candidate scenes very quickly. It's common to end up with a handful of scenes.

From Many Scenes to One

Next, we imagine that the director can only include one of those scenes in the movie.

If the client were to pick just one scene to best explain the hero's struggle, which scene do they feel is most impactful?

Notice the amount of choice and control the client has over this entire process. Not only are we leaning on their wisdom the whole way through, we are providing a framework that gives them the power of choice over the process.

The Movie Question provides the outline. The client provides the information.

We now have a scene that, in the client's view, best explains the dilemma that stands in the way of the change they want.

We can now use that scene to create something new and genuinely life changing.

An Imaginal Road Map

In the following pages, I will walk you through a road map of the imaginal protocol I developed. I created it from the ground up. I looked at the steps of memory reconsolidation and built this protocol from scratch. It's an example of the kind of innovation we are free to try once we understand what the brain needs in order to trigger trauma removal.

The protocol has four steps. Often, each step takes place in a different session. Yet, no client is the same. Some will move through the steps more quickly. Others will take a little longer. We move at the pace of the client.

The four steps are:

1. Identify the feelings from the original event.

2. List the feelings that the client wants to emerge with instead.

3. Build a new version of the scene that creates these new feelings.

4. Imaginally experience the new scene multiple times.

When explaining this protocol in more detail, I'll assume that each is a separate session. I will refer to each as session 1, session 2, session 3 and session 4.

Note that session 1 is not the first session in therapy itself. Just the first session of this protocol.

You will still need to do the kind of preparation I have already mentioned. By this stage, you will understand the client's problem and what they want instead. You will have identified a target learning that needs updating. The client will have selected a scene to work with.

Note that this protocol is simply one of many tools that can implement the update.

Before we look at the first session, I take it for granted that you already know how to ground your client if needed. Likewise, I assume that you already appreciate how to keep clients within their window of tolerance.

This is not a book about that, but those skills are needed in trauma work. It is important to know how to look after the client as they face things that are potentially distressing.

That said, clients will reach this part of the work once they have gained some key insights and aha moments. They have a much clearer understanding around their suffering. Armed with these insights, I notice that most clients are keen to do this work, and that the understanding gives them some power and distance that is itself somewhat protective.

Even so, you should not attempt this kind of work unless you already have knowledge of grounding techniques and other ways of taking care of a distressed client.

Let us take each session in turn.

CHAPTER 11

SESSION 1 - HARVESTING OLD FEELINGS

I n the first session of the four-part imaginal protocol, we focus on harvesting feelings.

We invite the client to reconnect with the chosen scene and notice the feelings that arise.

How was it for the client in that scene? How does it feel to reconnect there?

The feelings harvest covers the following categories of feelings:

1. Bodily sensations
2. Nervous system responses
3. Edited movements
4. Emotions
5. Felt sense of the situation

As I move through this process with the client, I like to write down their responses on a whiteboard (or electronic whiteboard).

Doing so gives us a shared record of their response to the selected scene. It also proves useful in the second session when we begin to build the change.

With these categories, there is no need to do the exercise in a linear fashion. In practice, the client will be sharing feelings that can come from any category.

Make sure that all categories are fully covered by the end of the harvesting.

Bodily Sensations

Invite the client to connect with what is happening in their body. As they reconnect to the selected scene, how is their body responding?

People report a range of bodily responses. For instance, a client may report stomach ache, tingly fingers, chest tightness, facial tightness, and nausea, amongst others.

Typically, the client will start by reporting the chief feeling that they notice. You can help them harvest more bodily responses by subtly walking them through a body scan.

Therapist: What do you notice about your body as you connect to this scene?

Client: My throat feels instantly tight.

Therapist: Okay, so you feel a tightness in your throat.

Client: Yes.

Therapist: And is there anything else going on too?

Client: Well, I can feel like a wave of nausea.

Therapist: Ah ok, that makes sense. Where are you feeling that?

Client: Well, it's kind of my stomach, but then it rises to my throat.

Therapist: Ok. So the nausea starts in the stomach but then rises to the throat where it feels tight.

Client: Yes.

Therapist: And how about your face? Is there anything happening there?

Client: Erm. I don't know. (pause) Yes, my jaw is tight, I suppose. Like clenched.

Therapist: Right, so the jaw is clenched.

Client: Yes.

Therapist: Anything in your chest?

Client: No, I don't think so. The chest feels ok.

Therapist: Okay. How about your limbs? Your arms and your legs.

Client: Well, my legs are kind of jumpy, I notice. And my fingers are tingling at the tips.

Therapist: Okay, you're doing really good. So, there's the tight throat. A wave of nausea from your stomach up to your throat. Your jaw feels clenched. Your legs are jumping and you can feel a tingle in your fingers.

Client: Yes, that's right.

Therapist: Anything more?

Client: No, I think that's it.

Through this questioning, we invite the client to fully harvest bodily sensations that could easily be overlooked.

The questions gently conduct a body scan. They help the client to discover the sensations that arise when they connect to the selected scene.

Nervous System Responses

Next, we ask about what their nervous system is doing.

When the nervous system notices signs of threat (or an absence of safety) it will either shut down or activate.

The shut down state will bring feelings of withdrawal, freezing, and numbing. It is the defence mechanism that happens when the problem seems unsolvable.

In nature, when a prey is caught by a predator and is unable to escape, this defence mechanism kicks in.

The numbing helps the creature not feel the full extent of the physical pain from the predator's attack.

The "play dead" appearance can sometimes make the predator lose interest and allow for an escape.

Similarly, the freeze response may protect a creature from being seen by a predator. The eye is particularly responsive to signs of movement. So, it makes sense that there is a defence mechanism that results in a freeze.

A client may report feeling "numb" or "frozen stiff" or "rooted to the spot". These are clues that the nervous system responds to the selected scene with signs of shut down.

Another possibility is that the nervous system moves into fight or flight, known as the sympathetic nervous system.

Unlike shut down, which slows us even to the point of freezing, the sympathetic nervous system speeds things up. The body begins to physically prepare to either fight or flee.

As such, the heart speeds up to get blood to the muscles. Adrenaline and other chemicals are released into the bloodstream.

The client may report physical sensations like increased heart rate, shortness of breath, sweating, blushing, or agitation. The term fight or flight makes sense to clients who experience this.

Edited Movements

During emotionally significant scenes, especially those that felt threatening, we can edit movements and actions.

We have already seen how the nervous system can take over and enforce a freeze response. In a freeze response, all actions, including potentially self protective ones, are not accessible.

Even without this freeze, we may be smart enough to understand that taking an action could make this awful situation unbearably worse.

Think of the six-year-old watching in terror as her father attacks her mother. Even if the freeze response does not activate, she knows that any intervention would only make Dad even more furious. So, cleverly, she edits herself and her movements.

In traumatic scenarios, this editing of motor impulses is common. The body freezes. Actions that we want to take don't feel safe to take. Things we want to say or yell out get strangled in the throat.

During this part of the session, we ask the client about any such editing.

Clients may report feeling frozen, or scared to move, or wishing they could yell "stop!"

There were often impulses to take an action, make a movement, or say something that could not be given life to.

Emotions

We know a lot about what is happening physically as a result of reconnecting to the selected scene.

We need to ensure that the client shares the emotional content too.

Clients may share that they felt overwhelmed, terrified, sad, furious, disappointed, resigned, or defeated, amongst other emotions.

It can sometimes be helpful to ask about the emotion behind the bodily sensations too.

Therapist: So the nausea you feel in your stomach, what is the emotion behind that? Is it fear? Sadness? Anger? A blend? Something else?

Client: It's sadness. Like a real deep pit of sadness.

When the client is struggling to identify the emotional content of a bodily sensation, checking these common emotions can help the client to connect.

I often ask: "Is it fear? Sadness? Anger? A blend? Something else?"

Clients are really good at identifying all kinds of sophisticated and subtle nuances of emotion.

Therapist: What are the emotions that come up for you?

Client: Oh I'm mad. I'm really angry.

Therapist: Yes, I get that. No wonder you feel so angry about this. Any other emotions there too?

Client: I'm not sure.

Therapist: How about that tightness in the throat you mentioned? What is the emotion behind that? Is it fear? Sadness? Anger? A blend? Something else?

Client: Oh it's terror. Utter terror.

Therapist: Yeah?

Client: It's like, "don't speak, don't make a sound!"

Therapist: Right. So, it's holding the words in.

Client: Yes, it's terrified in case I say something. Or even cry. So my throat is really tight trying to keep it in.

Notice how insights are occurring during this process too, not just feelings.

Felt Sense

There are some feelings that are not sensations and nor are they emotions.

Yet they represent a felt sense of the situation.

Sometimes, when using the word feel, we use it in such a way that it represents our instinctive, intuitive understanding of what was going on.

I will guide clients to notice their felt sense. In exploring this aspect, the client is able to unveil the meaning they ascribe to the traumatic event.

Therapist: One of the ways we can use feelings is to think about your felt sense. So, not emotions like sad or angry. And not bodily sensations, but words like trapped, for instance. That's not an emotion, but it's how a person might have felt in this situation. What is your felt sense of this scene? How did you feel?

Client: I felt worthless, completely unloved.

Therapist: Yes.

Client: I just felt like I didn't matter. Like, how could I matter if they did this to me?

Therapist: Yes, I get that. Those are big feelings. What else comes up for you?

Client: Well, you said trapped before. I did feel trapped. And I felt like I could never fix this problem. I felt like no one was ever going to listen to me.

Therapist: Yes.

Client: It felt unfair. Unjust. People shouldn't just be allowed to do this and get away with it.

As this exchange shows, the "felt sense" part of the exercise uncovers the meanings that the client gave to what happened.

Notice the meanings that this client has taken on in their life as a result:

- I am worthless.
- I am unloved / unlovable.
- I don't matter.
- I am trapped.
- Problems are not solvable.
- I am not listened to.
- Life is unfair.
- Life is unjust.

Checking the Harvest

Your whiteboard will now contain the feelings that are generated by connection to this scene.

Those feelings will cover:

- Bodily sensations
- Nervous system responses
- The editing of motor impulses
- Emotions
- Felt sense / meaning

You can use these descriptions to check whether these feelings show up for the client in present life too.

Therapist: So let's look at this list of feelings and responses to that old scene. And let's think of the issue that we are working on about what happens for you in romantic relationships. When you read this list, is this the same as what comes up for you in life today?

Client: Totally. Yes. That's exactly what happens. Whenever I feel that my partner has slighted me in some way, all of that comes up big time!

In this answer, the client can see that:

1. They selected the right scene to represent their current problem.
2. There is a link between these past events and today.
3. We are working on the right thing.

This check also allows us to pivot to a different scene if the link between the two is not established. In practice, such pivots are rarely needed. The client tends to have a great intuition for picking the right scene.

Summary

The first session of this protocol is where we dig into the scene and harvest the feelings associated.

We do this by ensuring that all of these categories are explored:

1. Bodily sensations
2. Nervous system responses
3. Edited movements and action
4. Emotions
5. Felt sense of the situation

This gives us the physical and autonomic responses. It allows us to identify actions and movements that were repressed in the original scene. It allows us to identify the emotions involved.

Finally, the felt sense gives us an insight into the meaning that the client attaches to the scene. It experientially accesses the client's beliefs about self, others, and the world.

In doing so, the client notices responses from the scene that will be very familiar for them. They will notice that the scene involves the same trauma responses that are interrupting life today.

CHAPTER 12

SESSION 2 - IDENTIFY OPPOSITE FEELINGS

At this stage, the client has now identified the feelings and meanings that are triggered when the trauma response kicks in.

In memory reconsolidation work, the aim is to identify the target learning that we want to neutralise - and then mismatch it.

In this case, the target learning is the list of feelings from the first session. In this, the second session, we identify the mismatch feelings.

Mismatch feelings will break the prediction of the nervous system. The nervous system expects that cues from the old scene will result in the trauma responses already identified.

Yet, the imaginal reenactment will give the nervous system different, mismatching responses instead.

This session helps the client to identify what those new feelings would be. As you will see, we use the information from session 1 as a jumping off point to create a list of mismatches.

The client knows that our work is leading up to eventually experiencing an imaginal reenactment scene. In this session, we ask what feelings they would like to emerge with from that scene.

We can do this by asking some form of the following question:

Therapist: Once this scene has been reimagined completely in your favour, what are the feelings that you want to emerge with instead?

When they reply, there are typically two stages:

1. The Freeform Phase
2. The Conscious Opposites Phase

Freeforming

Typically, the client will start listing new desired feelings right away. They do not need prompting at first. As they call out various desired feelings, make a note on a whiteboard that you can both see.

It will become apparent that the client has a clear idea of what they need. When developing these mismatches, I always advise leaning heavily on the client's wisdom.

Give space for the client to identify what they need. It can be tempting to add your own words to the list, but the process works best when you keep out of the way and merely guide the client.

Conscious Opposites

Eventually, their initial list of ideas will dry up. This is where the exercise can switch away from freeforming, and use the original feelings as a jumping off point.

Move through the list from our last session, and consciously seek opposites of them instead.

For instance, if the client has said that the old scene led to them feeling unloved, we can ask what they would need instead. This prompts the client to explore opposites, which would mismatch the original feeling.

In this instance, it is likely that the client will say that instead of feeling unloved, they would need to feel loved in the new scene.

Again, it is important to let the client use their own words. Sometimes the opposites are obvious - like unloved to loved, or unsafe to safe.

At other times, it is less clear. For instance, it is not immediately obvious what someone may want to feel instead of shame. Lean on the client. They know.

Restrict your role to that of guide and note taker.

Keep working through the list of original feelings. Ask the client what they would need instead from the new scene.

Remind them that these are the feelings they emerge with when a new scene goes entirely in their favour - a scene that meets their needs completely.

At this stage, we are not building that scene. We are only creating the desired feelings-based outcome.

Sometimes the client may rush ahead into the development of the new story. They may generate some ideas of what would happen in the new scene. They may even begin to get stuck around what needs to happen in the new scene.

Acknowledge and validate these initial ideas. Let them know that in the next session we will dig into how we get to these feelings as the outcome.

But for now, keep focused on just building the outcome. Reassure them that the scene building will be much easier when we know the feelings it is intended to generate.

From Absences to Presences

A useful role for the therapist is to help the client turn an absence of feeling into its positive, opposite instance.

For example, if a client feels scared in the original scene, they may say that in the new scene they want to not feel scared. This is a very common response during this session.

Clients will describe the new, desired feelings by simply adding the word 'not' to the original feeling. Scared becomes not scared. Ashamed becomes not ashamed.

Validate these responses. But then dig a little further until you have an instance of a new feeling.

For example: "So if you were not feeling anxious, what would you be feeling instead?"

This helps the client to identify the presence of something, perhaps calm.

To illustrate, here is an example dialogue between a therapist and client. At this point, they are working slowly through the original list of feelings one at a time.

Therapist: I notice on this list that you felt dismissed in the original scene.

Client: Yes.

Therapist: So in the new scene, what would you need to be feeling instead?

Client: (thinks) Well, I'd like to feel not dismissed I suppose.

Therapist: Yes. That makes sense. You'd like to not feel dismissed.

Client: Definitely.

Therapist: And if you were no longer feeling dismissed in the new scene, what would that feeling be instead?

Client: (thinks) Erm. I'm not sure. I'm just not wanting to feel dismissed anymore.

Therapist: Right. Because in the old scene, as it originally happened, you really did feel dismissed.

Client: Yes.

Therapist: And in this new scene, that feeling of being dismissed wouldn't be there because this scene will go completely in your favour.

Client: Yes. That's right.

Therapist: So if the feeling of being dismissed wasn't there - what feeling would be there in its place?

Client: Well, I think I'd feel heard. I'd feel like I was being taken into account. Like I mattered.

Therapist: Ah right. (On the shared whiteboard, the therapist notes down: Heard. Taken Into Account. I Matter.)

Example Outcome

By the end of the session, you will have two lists. First, a list of feelings describing how it was originally (session 1). Also, an opposite list of how the client wants to feel instead.

On the next page is an example of each, side by side.

THEN	AFTER NEW SCENE
Scared	Safe
Unloved	Loved
Dismissed	Heard
Ignored	Taken account of
Cheap	More than good enough
Like I didn't matter	I matter
Sad	Happy
Helpless	Content
Terrified	At ease
Shocked	Can make decisions
Confused	Powerful
Worthless	Strong
Not good enough	Clear, I know just what to do
Unwanted	High self esteem
Ashamed	Confident
Frozen	Proud
Stomach in knots	Precious
	Wanted
	I can use my voice
	Boundaried
	I state my needs
	Stomach feels relaxed and calm
	Breathing easy - slow, deep breaths

In the next session, we will use this new list as a guide. We will create a new scene that takes the cues of the distressing scene, yet delivers these mismatching outcomes.

Already Inviting Change?

Notice that this second session is more pleasant than session one. In the first session, the client was reconnecting with difficult feelings from the original scene.

In this session, the feelings being primarily connected to are more pleasant ones.

It is worth some speculation here as to whether memory reconsolidation could occur during this session, even though that is not our explicit goal.

You will notice that the client is continually leaping between the old target feelings to the new desired feelings.

The client is momentarily connecting to an old feeling, such as unsafe, unloved, or dismissed. Then immediately connecting to the opposite feeling, such as safe, loved, or heard.

This, in itself, is a repeated juxtaposition between the old and the new. When we connect to a sense of feeling unloved, there is typically some level of emotional activation. Likewise, connecting to feeling loved and wanted brings an emotional response too. The feelings of being loved and wanted mismatch the feeling of being unloved.

Some clients do report change after this second session. It is not the purpose of the session, so there is no need to create that expectation.

But it makes sense that some clients experience change from this repeated mismatching. Some people perhaps have a more experiential response to the process, even without being explicitly guided.

Recap

The main focus of this session is to gather the feelings that are wanted by the client. We will reverse engineer the new imaginal scene to ensure that it generates all of these new, mismatching feelings.

At first, we invite the client to freeform to generate those feelings. We ask what feelings they want from a new scene that is reimagined completely in their favour.

We do not yet focus at all on what that scene will be. We only seek to learn which feelings the client wants from the new scene.

This freeforming will generate a useful collection of outcome feelings.

Once this freeforming has run dry, we then consciously generate opposites to the feelings produced by the original scene.

Work through the original list gently and slowly, prompting the client for what they need instead.

Whenever the client merely describes the absence of a feeling, help them to describe the presence of what feeling will be there instead.

Even if they are describing the absence of a bodily sensation, such as a tightness in the chest, help them connect to the sensation of how the chest will feel once that tightness has gone.

"I'd no longer have a tight chest" becomes "my chest feels loose and free."

After all, just as we can't "not think of an elephant", the nervous system won't produce a calm response to "not terror". We need the new feelings to be instances of something, rather than a list of nots.

As in the last session, the kinds of feelings that we are looking to identify are:

- Bodily sensations
- Nervous system responses
- The release of edited motor impulses
- Emotions
- Felt sense / meaning

CHAPTER 13

SESSION 3 - BUILD
A NEW SCENE

From the previous two sessions, we now have the target feelings that we wish to replace, and the new feelings that we will replace them with.

In this session, we will co-create a new scene. It will be based upon the old scene, but refashioned completely in the client's favour. The new version of the scene will produce the new, desired feelings.

By the end of this session, the client will have a "first draft" scene. They will not directly experience this scene imaginally just yet. That will happen next time. They will simply design a scene that would produce the desired feelings.

This is a process of reverse engineering. We know the feelings we want to generate, so we create a scene to do that.

When co-creating a scene, it will not look like a script from a screenplay. It doesn't need to be so detailed. Rather, you will go through the new scene beat by beat. I'll show an example of this at the end of this chapter.

Although I describe this process as co-creation, in practice, the role of the therapist is minimal. The creation is rightly done by the client. The therapist merely facilitates the process.

It can be tempting for the therapist to have wonderful ideas and suggest them to the client. Resist that temptation and stay hands off. Your ideas aren't required and will likely get in the way. Just let the client build it beat by beat. Your client absolutely knows what they need.

I learned the importance of this by having (ahem) "better ideas" than my client at times. At these moments, I have been convinced that I know exactly what needs to happen in the scene.

Sharing these "better ideas" immediately revealed them to be worse ideas. So, I've learned to stop doing that. Invariably, the idea in my head turns out to be nowhere as good as what the client comes up with.

Sometimes clients may get stuck in the building of these scenes. The job of the therapist is to keep exploring. Connect the client to what they might need at that beat of the scene so they get the feelings they want.

Three Parts of Any Scene

A question that often arises is: what parts of the old scene do we reimagine? All of it, or just some of it?

I'll break it down so you can see which parts to keep, and which to change.

There are three parts to any scene:

A. Before the triggering event when all is well

B. The triggering event that made the safe become unsafe

C. Everything after that

Let me give an example that relates to bullying.

A. Before the triggering event when all is well

Sam is sitting in the corner of the playground happily munching on a sandwich and reading a book.

B. The triggering event that made the safe unsafe

This is the moment when the world is turned upside down. I often refer to this as the autonomic spark. It is the moment that the nervous system is triggered.

In this example, the bully and his two friends arrive, and the bully grabs Sam by the hair.

Notice how all was fine until the bully arrived and targeted Sam. This is the moment (and it really is a moment) of autonomic spark.

C. Everything after that

Now the ordeal begins where the bully attacks and humiliates Sam.

When generating a new version of the scene, we keep parts A and B, and reimagine part C completely in the client's favour.

There is a good reason for this. What we are looking for is to create a new response to the old trigger.

In current life, when the present resembles the traumatic incident, the nervous system responds today just as it did then.

The aim of the reconsolidation work is to ensure that the same cue produces new feelings and responses, not the ones which now get in the client's way.

In order to generate new responses to the old autonomic spark, we keep that autonomic spark in the new scene. We can then build a new set of responses to the same stimulus.

The client may at first seek to reimagine the entire scene away. In therapy, Sam may say: "In my new scene, the bully never comes and I just enjoy my sandwich in peace."

However, that doesn't activate the old brain pathway, and so won't create a new response to the old autonomic spark.

To have a new response, the reimagined scene will keep parts A and B.

But once the trigger occurs, the rest of the scene is reimagined in the client's favour. It plays out exactly how the client needs it to, and so generates new responses to the traumatic incident.

Breaking Down a Traumatic Scene

Let's look at another traumatic scene and break it down into these three parts:

    A. Before the triggering event when all is well

    B. The triggering event that made the safe unsafe

    C. Everything after that

A. Before the triggering event when all is well

Jack is listening to his favourite band on his earphones while on his daily walk.

B. The triggering event that made the safe unsafe

Suddenly, he is grabbed from behind and a stranger holds a knife to him and demands his wallet and his phone.

C. Everything after that

Jack hands over his valuables. The stranger threatens him with the knife once more and runs off, leaving Jack feeling shaken and upset.

When it comes to reimagining this scene, unpleasant as it is, we keep parts A and B.

The part we reimagine is everything after that.

Again, this is because we need a new response to the same old cues.

Think of Jack's life after this traumatising event. He is now too scared to go on walks. He no longer listens to his favourite band as he connects it to the trauma.

When he does go out, which is rare, he is on constant hyper-alert.

Jack needs new autonomic responses to these cues. His nervous system can then return to responding usefully in the here and now, rather than from past trauma.

Jack's new scene must still contain the part where he is enjoying his walk and listening to his favourite band. It must still contain the moment he is set upon. What changes is everything after that to get exactly the feelings he identified in session 2.

Our job is to guide the client to create the new scene that will reconsolidate the old trauma response.

Building the Reimagining Without Shame

In the new scene, the version of the client who suffered the traumatic event does not have to do anything different. What they did at the time was successful after all, as they survived the situation.

Their response, and the response of their nervous system, succeeded. Their job was to ensure the organism stayed alive. And it did.

Also, it is very likely that another response was simply not possible or sensible in that moment.

Think of a child in the midst of a traumatic event, for instance. The aim of any reimagining is not to have that child, as it was, to respond differently.

We are not revisiting the past but reimagining a copy of the scene, with new present-day resources.

As such, it is no longer that child's job. The version of the client from the original scene now has their current self with them. Their current self can ensure they have any resources, support, safety, or help that is needed.

Their response at the time was the correct one, as shown by the fact that they are still here.

But in this copy, with all of these additional resources, there is the opportunity for the client to get the feelings they need. In this copy, it can be different. Different responses are now possible within this safe, perfectly resourced copy.

In this reimagined scene, the client need not be limited by how it was back then. They can now reimagine the scene however they need so it generates the desired feelings.

It need not even be naturalistic. All that matters is that the nervous system believes it. Clients can grow in size, develop super strength, get superpowers, call on allies, or call on their own current self.

Or whatever. It doesn't matter, so long as the new desired feelings are generated.

This is an important point. It needs to be made clear that this is not a revisiting. Instead, it is a do-over with a copy of the old scene. In this copy, anything is possible.

This time, their current self can act as the "God" of the scene. Everything in the scene is like plasticine and can be changed at will.

Their younger self does not hold responsibility for making the scene different, even if in this copy new responses are now possible.

Instead, the current self holds that task. The current self plays with the scene so their younger self gets exactly what they need.

If it results in the younger self doing different things than they did, this is the gift of the new resources available within this copy. The current self is in charge of the scene. It is able to make new things possible and ensure it feels safe for these new things to happen.

What Do You Need to Happen Next?

The core question that the therapist offers to this process of reimagining is: "What do you need to happen next?"

This question will be repeated many times as you guide the client to create the new version of the scene.

Let's look at Jack's traumatic event. It may begin like this:

Therapist: So, we'll start this new scene as it originally was. You are walking. And you are listening to your favourite music. Then suddenly this guy grabs you. In order to get these new feelings that you want, what do you need to happen next?

This begins the process.

Keep the list of desired feelings available for the client to see and refer to. After all, they are now creating a scene with the explicit aim of generating those feelings.

From time to time, have the client check in with the list as the new scene is being created. Then you can ask that core question again:

Therapist: So in order to get these feelings, what do you need to happen next?

Being Interactional

In any scene that begins to play out, check out how others in the scene are responding.

For example, in this example of a client confronting her violent father:

Therapist: So what do you need to happen now?

Client: I tell him to cut it out. I tell him it is hurting me to see this and that I want it to stop!

Therapist: Wow. Yes. So you tell him to cut it out. It's hurting you and you want it to stop.

Client: Yes.

Therapist: And when you say that, is there a response from him? If there is, what do you need that to be? What do you need to happen next?

Client: Well, I'd need him to actually hear that.

Therapist: Right. You need to be heard.

Client: Yes.

Therapist: So if he was to hear you at that moment like you need, how would you know he was hearing you?

Client: Well, he'd kind of come to his senses. Like it would bring him out of himself.

Therapist: And what lets you know that he's come to his senses in the way you need him to? What do you notice?

Client: Well, it's like a light bulb moment and you can just see he's not angry Dad anymore.

Therapist: I see. So you can see he's not angry Dad anymore. You've told him what you need and how this is affecting you, and he has come to his senses.

Client: Yes. He's come to his senses. He's back to normal again.

Therapist: And so what do you need to happen next?

Client: I need him to own it. I need him to make sure it stops.

Therapist: So what would you need him to say so that you knew for sure that this was going to stop?

This is only part of the scene building in this case. But notice the emphasis on meeting needs.

In this short exchange, the therapist has asked the following:

- What do you need to happen now / next?
- What response from Dad do you need?

- If he was to hear you like you need, how would you know?
- What would you need him to say so you knew for sure that this was going to stop?

Also, notice the emphasis on specificity.

The client expresses a need to be heard. Help them connect to what that would look like if that need is met.

"If he was to hear you like you need, how would you know?"

This kind of question can be used for any need. For instance, a client who needs to feel strong and confident:

"So if you were strong and confident in this scene right now, what would you be noticing about yourself?"

The following kind of questions all help to make the scene specific:

- How would you know?
- What would you notice?
- What would it look like?
- What would you / they be doing?
- What would you notice yourself / them saying?

Sometimes the client will be in a scene and say something like "I need a hug". Make it specific. Ask: "Who would you like the hug from?"

As the client gets their needs met in this re-creation, you can check in with how it feels.

Therapist: And what do you need to happen next?

Client: I think I just need to be hugged.

Therapist: Yeah. You need to be hugged. Who do you need to be hugged by when you get that hug?

Client: Erm. I think maybe Grandma.

Therapist: So you'd like to be hugged by Grandma.

Client: Yes.

Therapist: And does that feel good to be hugged by Grandma?

Client: Yes, it feels really safe.

Therapist: Yes. It feels safe being hugged like that by Grandma.

Client: Yes.

Therapist: What do you notice about how Grandma hugs you that makes it feel so safe?

Again, this exchange is about:

- What they need to happen next
- How they would know it is happening
- Generating specificity

When The Naturalistic Does Not Feel Believable

I mentioned earlier how scenes don't need to be naturalistic. All that matters is that they are believable.

A client can gain the ability to fly like Superman, or be able to literally shrink the scary person to the size of a thumb - and it feels totally believable.

Yet a naturalistic event can occur that the client rejects completely. They may need a hug from Mum. But receiving it does not feel believable at all.

Before the process starts, I invite clients to choose who is in the scene. It may well have been their own parents in the original scene. But it needn't be in the new scene.

Some clients like to swap them out.

For instance, when little, Veronica suffered a violent assault from an older gang while out playing. She was thrown to the floor and dragged and kicked.

When she runs home in tears, her mother provides no comfort in the wake of the attack. Instead, she beats Veronica for the rip in her dress.

In the new scene, Veronica desperately needs that hug still, but she simply cannot imagine her mother offering it. If she went ahead with it anyhow, she would only reject it. It would kill the believability of the scene and would not produce the desired feelings. Remember, producing the desired feelings is the point.

So, at the start of the session, I ask Veronica who she would like to be in the scene. Does she need it to be her own parents or would she like to have imaginal parents instead?

The therapist can never know the answer. Asking the question is enough. The client knows what they need, so feel free to lean on that expertise.

In this case, Veronica chose to swap out her own mother with the kind of mother she needed. As such, she was able to run home and get the love and care she needed from a mother figure that she could believe in.

Recapping the Flow of the Story

As the client shares what they need, the therapist makes a note of each beat of the story. I typically do this with asterisks as bullet points (see the example later).

From time to time, I'll recap the story from the beginning. This gives the client some time to follow the flow. It makes it easier for them to know what they need to happen next. It only takes a moment, but is very useful to do from time to time.

Completing the Scene

There will come a point where the scene looks like it may be complete. There is an element of using your instinct here. Like when watching TV or going to the theatre, it just feels like the job of that scene is done.

Often, there are markers such as a culmination hug, or the client continues with the day happily.

Still, it is only a therapist's guess, so gently check it out.

When you notice that the scene may be completed, you can ask if it feels complete or if more needs to happen to make it complete.

Therapist: And what do you need to happen next?

Client: I think we all just hug. It feels nice. We are all together again.

Therapist: Yes, that sounds lovely. And does this scene feel complete to you, or is there anything more that needs to happen for you?

Client: Yes, I just start to play. I'm a kid again and I'm able to just be a kid.

Therapist: Right. And do you need to play for a bit in the scene or is that the end?

Client: (smiling) No. That's the end.

A Worked Example

I will now show an illustration of the beats of such a re-created scene. This will help you to see what we have by the end of the session.

In this case, in the original scene, it is Donna's ninth birthday and she has dressed up expecting to be taken to a birthday treat that her mother has promised her.

Donna is very excited, yet it turns out to be a lie designed to build Donna's hopes up. Instead, Donna's mother mocks her and has her spend the day cleaning the basement at the home of her recently deceased Grandma, who Donna adored.

When Donna cries, her mother beats her and tells her she doesn't deserve a birthday treat. Donna spends the rest of her birthday in the basement.

When she connects to the original scene she felt: scared, unloved, dismissed, ignored, cheap, like she didn't matter, sad, helpless, terrified, shocked, confused, worthless, not good enough, unwanted, ashamed, frozen, stomach in knots.

Instead, she wants to feel: safe, loved, heard, taken account of, good enough, that she matters, happy, content, at ease, can make decisions, powerful, strong, clear, she knows exactly what to do, high self esteem, confident, proud, precious, wanted, I can use my voice, boundaried, I state my needs, my stomach feels relaxed and calm, my breathing takes easy slow deep breaths.

By the end of the session, these are the beats of the new scene that Donna has created:

- Donna is excited and dressed up for the treat Mum promised her.

- She arrives at Grandma's house and feels puzzled.

- Mum reveals that there's no birthday treat and mocks Donna (the autonomic spark event - everything afterwards can be changed).

- Donna outright refuses to go into the basement.

- Mum gets angrier but Donna stands upright and shouts "No! You can't treat me like this anymore!"

- Donna gives Mum a fierce stare that shrinks Mum to the size of a thimble.

- Mum is still angry, but with a squeaky voice and Donna finds her funny.

- Her Grandma then appears in the scene and sides with Donna.

- Grandma is cross that Mum treated Donna this way and tells Mum off.

- Grandma puts thimble sized Mum in her purse "where she can't cause any more trouble" and Donna giggles.

- Grandma hugs Donna and tells her that she is a lovely little girl who deserves a real birthday treat.

- Suddenly Grandma pulls back a curtain and all Donna's friends are there and are cheering and singing happy birthday.

- There are balloons and presents and party food.

- Grandma asks Donna what would make it even better and Donna says she wants to blow out her birthday candles and make a wish.

- Donna wishes that Lesley Judd from the TV show Blue Peter was her mum and suddenly Lesley Judd is there.

- Her new mum tells Donna that she is a wonderful little girl and that she is so lucky that Donna wished for her.

- Her new mum hugs Donna and kisses her on the head.

- The scene shifts to Donna being in her new bedroom and Lesley Judd, her new mum, is tucking her in and reading her a bedtime story, and Donna snuggles in and falls asleep.

I check with Donna to make sure that this scene would give her all of the feelings she needs:

- Safe
- Loved
- Heard
- Taken account of
- More than good enough
- I matter
- Happy
- Content
- At ease
- Can make decisions
- Powerful
- Strong
- Clear, I know just what to do
- High self esteem
- Confident
- Proud
- Precious
- Wanted
- I can use my voice

- Boundaried
- I state my needs
- Stomach feels relaxed and calm
- Breathing easy - slow, deep breaths

She confirms that she believes it will.

Summary

In this session, we are building the scene, but not yet experiencing it explicitly. The full imaginal experience will happen next time.

Nonetheless, there is a lot of imaginal labour taking place here. Again, clients can sometimes report some changes just from this session.

Even though they have not undergone the full imaginal experience, some clients receive the repeated juxtaposition necessary to overwrite trauma.

Remember that the brain needs ACTIVATION + MISMATCH + REPEAT.

As the client connects to how it was (activation) and mismatches it with how they need it to be, there can sometimes be enough here to reconsolidate. Again, that is not the aim of this session and it need not be expected.

Here are twelve key takeaways to help you do this work in practice:

1. The job of the new scene is to reverse engineer the desired feelings from the previous session.

2. Keep out of the way. Their ideas are better than the therapist's so lean exclusively on their wisdom.

3. The new scene will keep the autonomic spark event, and reimagine what follows.

4. The client's current self is in charge of making changes to the scene.

5. It is not the job of the client's younger self.

6. We are working with an imaginal copy where everything is plasticine and, here, it can be made safe to have different responses.

7. It doesn't have to be naturalistic, it just has to be believable.

8. Reality is sometimes less believable. Let the client swap people out if they'd prefer it.

9. The core question is: what do you need to happen next?

10. Scenes and stories are interactional. Help facilitate the to and fro between people in the scene, so that each responds to the other.

11. Specificity: help the client to flesh out what would be happening if an expressed need was being met.

12. The client decides when the scene is complete.

Of course, the scene created in this session may still change. It is only a first draft. When the client tries it on for size, they may well want to tweak it in various ways.

But for now, we have gone from:

1. The unpleasant feelings generated in the original scene
2. The desired feelings they want to emerge with instead
3. A draft scene designed specifically to meet their needs and generate these new feelings

In the next chapter, we will look at how to facilitate the full imaginal experience.

CHAPTER 14

EXPERIENCE THE NEW SCENE IMAGINALLY

So far, we have laid the groundwork for the imaginal experience that is to come. We now have:

- The feelings from the original event
- The opposite feelings that the client wants instead
- A first draft reenactment scene

In this session, the client gets to have the imaginal experience itself. In this chapter, I will show you how to facilitate this imaginal experience. I will cover the steps needed to ensure that memory reconsolidation is triggered and that trauma is overwritten for good.

There are several stages to this part of the work:

1. Reactivating the original event response
2. Trying on the reenactment scene

3. Checking whether the new scene created the desired feelings

4. Facilitating tweaks in order to get to a bullseye scene

5. Repeating the bullseye scene

Reactivating the Old

The equation of memory reconsolidation is:

ACTIVATE + MISMATCH + REPEAT = OVERWRITE

This is true of any resource we might use. Unless there is some activation of the original learning, you will fail to trigger memory reconsolidation.

Activating the original learning tells the brain which pathway to write onto. Without this activation, the brain puts the responses from the new scene into a different brain pathway.

Anatomically, we would be keeping the trauma intact, and creating some counteractive learning to compete with it. This ensures that relapse remains an option.

Only by activating the old learning (and mismatching it) do we open the trauma pathway for rewriting.

As such, begin this session by inviting the client to very briefly reactivate the original feelings. It only needs to be a light activation, so it takes just a couple of minutes. There is no need to go too deep into the original trauma response.

Therapist: So before we try out this new scene, I'd like you to briefly reconnect with the original feelings from back then.

The feelings you identified at the start of this work. Is that okay with you?

The client will then place their attention - very briefly - on the original event and the associated feelings.

Therapist: Are you feeling some of that?

Client: Yes, my chest is getting that tight feeling it gets.

Therapist: Okay. So that's enough. You can come back to me now. That's activated and so the brain now knows where to put this new information. Good work. How are you doing?

Client: Yeah, I'm good. I'm okay.

Trying on the Reenactment Scene

Now that the original response is activated, we are ready to help the client try on the reenactment scene that they created in the last session.

The therapist checks in with the client that they are ready to have this new experience. When they confirm that they are, it is a good idea to verbally recap the scene for them. This helps them reconnect to the scene they built and is a useful memory aid.

It also allows any last-minute tweaks.

Therapist (after recapping the new scene): So, have I remembered that right?

Client: Yes.

Therapist: And that's the new scene you'd like to experience today?

Client: Yes, except I'd like Auntie Dawn to hold my hand when we are in the car.

Therapist: Okay, lovely. So Auntie Dawn will hold your hand in the car.

Client: Yes.

Therapist: Anything else?

Client: No, everything else is good.

The client is now ready to experience the scene. The word experience is apt. When clients get into it, even though it is imagined, they often respond spontaneously to the experience.

They sometimes make changes during the scene itself. These moments feel right and so they make them happen during the imaginal experience itself. It is a testament to just how immersive these experiences are.

As I invite clients into the new scene, I tell them that this sometimes occurs. There may be moments as they live this new, imaginal experience that they want to respond to. I offer full permission to do so.

This is important. We don't want clients to feel locked into the imaginal scene they drafted. We want it to be a free, spontaneous process. I remind them that the scene we created was just a draft. If it feels right to do something else in the scene, feel free to do it.

For instance, one client had the urge to stand up within the imaginal scene, give full voice to his feelings, and walk out. So he did so.

It was a key moment. It wasn't in the scene they had originally drafted. But he gave himself the freedom to respond as needed during the experience.

It is worth restating that clients know what they need in these experiences. Offering full permission to respond in the moment within the scene is helpful.

I also remind clients that they can stop the scene at any point. They are in control, and that includes opening their eyes and reconnecting with me at any time.

This doesn't tend to happen often, but it's an important safety exit nonetheless.

When ready, I invite the client to close their eyes if they feel safe to do so. Closing their eyes helps them be in the imaginal scene more easily. If they don't feel safe to close their eyes, I guide them to find a spot to focus on instead.

I invite them to take their time, to not rush, but fully have the experience. When they are done, they can simply open their eyes again to finish.

Then, usually with eyes closed, they begin the scene. The scene has been built so it begins as it originally was, and then switches to fully meet the client's needs instead.

The therapist is completely silent at this point, merely waiting for the client to have the experience of their new scene.

I notice that, on average, clients spend about six minutes within the scene. Some take longer and others do it more quickly.

Checking the Scene

The new, imagined scene is just a device. Its role is to evoke the new opposite feelings from the same initial cues.

On rare occasions, a client has mentioned that they had difficulty with the imagery of the scene. Yet, they could feel the new positive feelings.

There is no need to force the imagery in such a case, as the scene is still doing its job - to evoke the new feelings.

In the aftermath of their first experience of this new scene, check in with them. Typically I will ask: "So how was that for you?"

This gives the client a platform to share what happened and whether it was a good experience for them.

I will ask whether anything new happened in the moment or whether it was pretty much the scene that they had designed.

Again, this allows the client to share any spontaneous moments that occurred.

Therapist: So, how was that for you?

Client: Yes. Good.

Therapist: And was the scene exactly as you had designed? Or did you notice other things happening too?

Client: Oh, well I did change one aspect, yes.

Therapist: Ok great. What was the change?

Client: Well, you know when Mum tried to beat me and I chose to stand up to her?

Therapist: Yes.

Client: Well, I had my brother with me in that part. Mum was always more wary of my brother.

Therapist: Ok great. So that felt safer?

Client: Yes.

Once the client has had a chance to debrief the experience, we can check whether the scene did the job it was designed for.

In session two of this protocol, the client described the new feelings that the scene is designed to provide. We can now go through those feelings like a checklist to see if it did.

One of two things will happen here. Often, the scene they created hits a bullseye. You move through the checklist of each wanted feeling, and they report that the scene fully produces every one. If this occurs, there is no need for further tweaking. I call this a bullseye scene.

Alternatively, the client will notice that the scene was successful for most, but not all, of those desired feelings. When this occurs, guide the client to tweak the scene so they get what they need.

Here is an example of moving through the checklist of a scene that only did most of the job, so is not yet a bullseye scene.

Therapist: Did you feel loved in this scene?

Client: Yes.

Therapist: Did you feel confident?

Client: Oh yes!

Therapist: Powerful?

Client: Yes!

Therapist: Did you feel safe?

Client: Well, yes, I guess.

Therapist: Ok, so there's some doubt there?

Client: Well, yes. I felt safe, but also wondered if my standing up to her was storing up some trouble. Like I'd pay for it later.

Therapist: Ah yes, that makes sense.

Tweaking the Scene

This check in allows the client to share any discomfort or fears that showed up. It allows them to identify where the scene missed its target, or only scored a partial win.

When the client reports anything that is short of fully hitting its target, we can deal with it right away by verbally reconstructing the scene even more in their favour.

Ask the client how they need the scene to be different in order to fully give them that desired feeling.

You can see why I regard the first attempt at an imaginal scene as just a first draft. It often changes. The change occurs either spontaneously during the experience itself, or as a result of noticing that there are gaps in what the scene achieved.

Let's pick up the conversation again with the client who stood up to Mum.

Therapist: Did you feel safe?

Client: Well, yes, I guess.

Therapist: Ok, so there's some doubt there?

Client: Well, yes. I felt safe, but also wondered if my standing up to her was storing up some trouble. Like I'd pay for it later.

Therapist: Ah yes, that makes sense.

Client: It was good to stand up to her. And it helped to have my brother with me. But once I left, I still felt kind of scared for the trouble it might have gotten me into.

Therapist: Right, I get that. So it didn't feel fully safe yet.

Client: That's right.

Therapist: So what would you need to be different in this scene for you to feel fully safe?

The client will then come up with an answer, or share their difficulties in finding an answer. Either way, you can help the client think this through without putting your own ideas in the way.

It is a genuinely powerful experience for the client to ponder and fix the scene in their own favour, guided by their innate connection to what they most need.

Each time the client reports a shortfall in creating a desired feeling, we deal with it in the same way.

In a different example below, the client wants to feel loved in the new scene, but it hasn't succeeded in creating that feeling.

Therapist: I see. So you didn't feel loved still in this scene?

Client: No, not really.

Therapist: So what needs to happen in this scene that might give you that feeling of being loved?

Client: I think I'd just need someone to sit with me and see that I was alright.

Therapist: Yes, of course. This was tough on you and you want someone to see that you're okay.

Client: Yeah.

Therapist: And who would you like that to be?

Client: Erm. Either Mum or Ruth from next door.

Therapist: I see, so you'd like either Mum or Ruth to check in on how you are.

Client: Yes. That would help a lot.

Therapist: Who would you prefer to be doing that? Mum or Ruth?

Client: I'd prefer Mum.

Therapist: Okay, yes. So in this new version of the scene, Mum is going to come and sit with you and see that you're okay.

Client: Yes.

Therapist: And will that result in you feeling loved? Or do you need something else to happen too?

Client: Maybe a hug.

Therapist: A hug from Mum?

Client: Yeah, I'd like a hug from Mum and for her to tell me that she loves me and it's going to be alright.

Make these tweaks in the same way for all feelings that the scene failed to fully evoke. The scene is redrafted to fill these gaps.

Trying on the Tweaked Scene

As before, the client is invited to close their eyes or find a fixed point. They will then imaginally experience the new, tweaked version of the scene.

Again, the therapist is completely silent. The therapist simply waits for the client to open their eyes at the end of the imaginal experience.

204 | How To Remove Trauma Response

At the end of the scene, check in again. Ask for spontaneous changes that may have shown up. Ask how it was for the client to experience the scene. Go through the checklist. If needed, tweak the scene and try it on again.

Keep going through this redrafting process until you end up with a bullseye scene that provides everything they needed.

A bullseye scene provides a mismatch that breaks the brain's prediction. The scene initially looks exactly as it did back then. The brain predicts the same threats and dangers so expects the client to feel just as bad.

Yet instead, the same beginning leads to the total satisfaction of the client's needs. Rather than the predicted danger and helplessness, there is a mismatch experience of safety and empowerment.

Triggering Reconsolidation

A mismatch experience is essential, but it is not enough to replace the old trauma with the new feelings.

A mismatch opens the brain pathway to be writable again. But it does no more than that. It is the metaphorical equivalent of unlocking the safe.

At this point, the safe is now open, but nothing has yet happened to the contents.

To overwrite a trauma response, the brain needs a mismatch experience to be repeated. Remember the formula:

ACTIVATE + MISMATCH + REPEAT = OVERWRITE.

We must repeat that clash of prediction and prediction error. We need to reactivate the old expectation and deliver the mismatch scene.

Think of our metaphor of the conker fight. One conker is the original learning (the prediction). The other conker is the mismatch experience (the prediction error).

A conker fight has these two conkers bump against each other, and keep doing so repeatedly. Memory reconsolidation works the same way.

One way to do this is to simply repeat the new bullseye scene.

Why This Works

Repeating the good experience works well for this particular approach. But it is worth noting that we can't always just repeat a good experience and achieve reconsolidation.

Repeating a good experience on its own is just one conker. Memory reconsolidation demands both:

- The original learning that forms the basis of the prediction
- AND the new mismatching experience

If we simply repeated a pleasant, guided imaginal experience where you enjoyed a beach scene, this would be nice, but it wouldn't be expected to trigger reconsolidation.

It just so happens that the bullseye scene inherently contains both the prediction and the mismatch. Not all approaches do.

There are three parts to any scene:

    A. Before the triggering event when all is well

    B. The triggering event that made the safe unsafe

    C. Everything after that

Our bullseye scene keeps parts A and B. When the client reimagines the new scene, they re-experience A and B as it originally was. This produces a prediction of distress.

Yet what occurs instead is a new outcome that meets all of the client's needs. Prediction and prediction error occur within the one experience.

Every time the client experiences the bullseye scene, they activate that old prediction while disconfirming it.

It is not merely a pleasant experience - it incorporates both activation and mismatch.

Repeating the Bullseye

We ask the client to go back into the bullseye scene. We fall silent and wait.

Then do it again.

I typically ensure that the client has experienced the bullseye version of the scene three times. This means we satisfy the equation of ACTIVATE + MISMATCH + REPEAT.

It ensures that they don't just have the mismatch, but they have the repetition as well.

The brain has now received what it needs to overwrite the old trauma response. That old set of cues now trigger a new prediction of safety. The trauma response is gone.

Summary

We have covered the steps of how to facilitate an imaginal reenactment.

As well as detailing each stage of the four-part process, we saw how it met the equation of memory reconsolidation. That equation is ACTIVATE + MISMATCH + REPEAT = OVERWRITE.

It is only by triggering memory reconsolidation that the unwanted trauma response is overwritten for good.

We saw how the final session involves five different elements:

1. Reactivating the original event response
2. Trying on the reenactment scene
3. Checking whether the new scene created the desired feelings
4. Facilitating tweaks in order to get to a bullseye scene
5. Repeating the bullseye scene

As you can see, this imaginal protocol follows the steps of memory reconsolidation.

It is an effective protocol and clients report that it is transformative. It guides the brain into overwriting the old trauma responses with something else entirely.

CHAPTER 15

TROUBLESHOOTING IMAGINAL WORK

If This Work Goes Beyond One Session

Sometimes session 4 of the protocol takes longer than one actual session. This needs to be managed.

Once a mismatch experience has occurred, that brain pathway is open for rewrite. It stays open for four to five hours. This gives time to repeat the experience and overwrite the trauma response.

Check out the implementation steps below:

1. Reactivate the target learning.
2. Activate the mismatch.
3. Repeat steps 1 and 2.

If you have done steps 1 and 2 and run out of time, what then? The brain pathway is open, but you don't have the time to repeat the experience.

By the time you next meet, the brain pathway will have locked shut again with the old trauma response intact.

This can feel frustrating for you as a therapist. You were one step away from transformational change and the clock intervened.

Independent Repetition

Let me begin with a reassurance. Memory reconsolidation (and the steps of memory reconsolidation) do not require a therapist.

A skilled therapist can ensure it happens sooner than it otherwise would. They may even ensure it happens when it otherwise never would.

But memory reconsolidation is simply how your client's brain works - and yours for that matter.

So, anything that hits the three implementation steps above would trigger memory reconsolidation.

I say this because it is possible that the client will repeat the experience independently.

Think of a time when someone said something so profound that it fundamentally changed your way of seeing. You saw the world one way and then suddenly that world view was turned upside down.

Did you then go about your day without giving it another thought? No, of course not. The brain pays special attention to such things.

For hours afterward you will be playing conkers in your own head, knocking the old truth up against the new one.

I believe that clients do this too. Next time you meet the client, it is a good idea to do some verification work to see if memory reconsolidation has taken place. I'll talk about how to do verification work a little later.

It is possible that the repetition step has happened independently of you, despite the fact that you ran out of time.

If the client took this profound experience and played mental conkers with it during the next few hours, they are completing the repetition step without you.

What Needs to Be Repeated and What Does Not

If you check in with your client, and you realise that memory reconsolidation has not taken place, what then?

It raises the question of what parts of the work need to be repeated? Do you need to repeat everything?

Must you go back and start session 1 from scratch? Thankfully, the answer is no. The preparation work never needs to be repeated. After all, once you have the ingredients, you already have them.

The brain isn't at all interested in how you gather the ingredients, just as the pan doesn't care how you chop the onions.

If you ran out of time last session, you only need to restart the implementation steps:

1. Ask the client to reconnect to how it was in the original scene so as to briefly reactivate the old feelings.

2. Invite them to experience the bullseye scene that is reimagined in their favour.

3. Have them experience this bullseye scene two more times.

The bullseye scene contains the prediction of bad feelings and the delivery of good feelings. Each time the client experiences the bullseye scene it repeats the activation and the mismatch.

The client completes the implementation stage of the work within the four to five hour window – albeit a session later than planned.

Memory reconsolidation is likely to occur.

When the Client Doesn't Want to Revisit a Childhood Scene

In the imaginal protocol just described, the client had chosen a memory from their past. This memory is representative of the trauma response that still gets in the way of life.

We asked the client to identify a scene from life that explains how they learned this response.

Like picking a scene from a movie, the client connects to a scene from their own life history that explains how these beliefs and nervous system responses were formed.

We then go through four stages to change that response:

1. Harvest the feelings and responses from that old scene.

2. Identify the opposite feelings and responses that are desired instead.

3. Create a version of that same scene that will be reimagined completely in the client's favour.

4. Imaginally experience that scene repeatedly.

This is a very effective approach at giving the brain what it needs to trigger the process of memory reconsolidation.

But there can be some problems with it as laid out.

In this chapter, you will realise that adherence to any particular method is not necessary. Rather, you will learn that memory reconsolidation work allows you flexibility and creativity.

By staying true to the core principles of memory reconsolidation, you will be able to pivot and find flexible, respectful responses to difficulties that arise in the work.

For instance, what if the client is unwilling to revisit the original trauma? What if it is simply too distressing to venture back there?

Similarly, what if the client simply can't remember a scene clearly? They experience their memory as fragmented, and so find that a scene doesn't come to them.

In each of these scenarios, it is not possible to access an original scene, and for good reason.

Thankfully, it is not essential to return to an old or original scene. Many clients do prefer to, as it gives them a sense of deeper understanding. But the brain does not need them to.

Keeping what the brain needs at the front of your mind will allow you a lot of flexibility in terms of how you trigger memory reconsolidation.

Remember, the key equation of memory reconsolidation:

ACTIVATE + MISMATCH + REPEAT = OVERWRITE

The brain demands that the trauma response is reactivated. This lets the brain know which brain pathway it is dealing with. Then, when the mismatch occurs, the brain knows to make that specific pathway rewritable.

This, anatomically, is key to trauma removal. Otherwise, the new information is not an overwrite but placed in a completely different brain pathway. The trauma response is kept intact, ready to be retriggered at any point.

The brain needs that trauma response to be activated. Yet, it is not specific as to how. It does not stipulate that we can only activate it with one specific, given scene.

Rather, activation of the trauma response is enough.

Of course, finding and revisiting an old scene where this trauma response was first learned will indeed reactivate it.

But so, too, do lots of things in the client's life. After all, if present day life was no longer activating this trauma response, the client would not be seeking your help. It would just be part of the archaeology of their history. It would not be touching life today.

The fact that they are seeking help is a sign that it is indeed touching life today.

For instance, the person who feels suddenly unsafe and yells at their partner is experiencing their trauma response in the here and now.

Similarly, think of the socially anxious person who wants to be able to relax around strangers and chat freely with them.

When they approach someone in present life, their nervous system kicks in and they withdraw into silence and freeze.

These are reactivations of the trauma response.

They don't need to consciously revisit their "origin story" to reactivate the trauma response. Life already does that on a week by week, day by day basis.

As such, if a client does not wish to revisit an old scene, you can find a recent one.

Therapist: So tell me about a time in the last week or so that this showed up for you.

Client: Well, I'm a manager at my job. A member of my team approached me asking me to do part of their work. I wanted to say no because it's their job and I'm already overwhelmed with my own work. But I just couldn't face the confrontation of saying no. And now I'm doing it.

Therapist: Right, so that's a great example.

Client: Yes, this is what always happens for me. Now I'm staying after work for hours and I notice them chatting to other people in the office because they have given their work to me. All because I was too scared to say no.

This recent scene has reactivated their trauma response. It does not feel safe for them to say no and risk the possible confrontation.

If we ask them to revisit this scene (as they have just, in fact, been able to do), then the protocol will work just as well.

We could even have them use their imagination to move the reel forward. What is the scene they worried would happen if they had said no to taking on the other person's tasks? We can ask the client to connect with how that confrontation with their team member may have played out.

This confrontation that did not even occur will also be activating.

Using The Core Equation of Memory Reconsolidation

The equation of memory reconsolidation is ACTIVATE + MISMATCH + REPEAT = OVERWRITE.

This recent scene, when revisited, activates the trauma response as adequately as an old scene. The feared response of their team member does too. So, either or both can be used.

Note that there is no need for high intensity of the trauma response. Memory reconsolidation is not more or less effective based on the intensity of the reactivation.

There are clinical approaches that deliberately set out to limit the intensity of the reactivation. For instance, Flash-type techniques in EMDR or the Rewind Technique. They do this to help clients stay within their window of tolerance.

For instance, the Four Blinks approach developed by Thomas Zimmerman uses a container to store the distress, in a deliberate attempt to keep it out of awareness. The effectiveness of these approaches help us to understand that light activation is sufficient.

As such, if a client does not want to return to an old scene, it is not necessary to use an old scene. A recent scene that represents a reactivation of the trauma should still be effective.

Indeed, Goran Hogberg's protocol, discussed earlier, resulted in astounding and lasting trauma removal. Yet, the reactivation triggered by Hogberg predominantly used source material from the past week.

Keep the core formula in mind: ACTIVATE + MISMATCH + REPEAT.

This core formula is much more important in your work than the specific rules of any particular techniques that you might read about here.

The core formula allows you to respond flexibly to blocks that the client may put up, or to time pressures within your session.

You can fully respect your client's choices and still find a way to trigger the transformational change they desire.

I recall the first time a client expressed an unwillingness to return to an old scene. If I had kept to the "rules" of the "system" I would have been stumped.

But I focused on the core formula of memory reconsolidation.

I knew the first step was to ACTIVATE and so I simply asked the client if they would be comfortable with a recent scene instead.

Likewise, I recall working with a client who had a very low window of tolerance. In this case, I asked the client to work with a recent scene where the distress was limited to a level of three out of ten.

This ensured that we were able to do the same work successfully, but with a lightly triggering recent event instead.

When therapists first encounter memory reconsolidation, it is easy to get hung up on the rules of the various techniques that are already out there.

But those rules are only useful because they follow the core formula. You can break those rules and be successful, so long as you meet the requirements of that simple equation.

Focus instead on the core formula that describes what the brain needs. When you do, you will find yourself free to create and be flexible in your approach.

Indeed, the very protocol I have described here is just my own creative response to the formula.

I asked myself how I could activate the trauma response, mismatch it, and then repeat that mismatch.

I came up with this approach as one of many possible answers.

Using the same creativity and flexibility, I work with many other approaches too.

By connecting to the core formula of memory reconsolidation, it allows me to identify those approaches that appear to meet its requirements.

It also enables me to tweak approaches which don't quite meet the requirements, but would with some amendment.

The work of memory reconsolidation informed therapists is one of creativity and flexibility.

We must activate the response, mismatch it and repeat the mismatch.

How we arrive at that destination offers perhaps an infinite number of possibilities.

A member of my Memory Reconsolidation Coaching Academy demonstrated this recently.

This therapist was relatively new to memory reconsolidation. She decided to try out some of her learning by using a particular approach with a client.

Her aim was to activate, mismatch, and repeat.

At some point during the session, she realised that time pressures would not permit her to complete her original plan.

Yet, she held the core formula of memory reconsolidation in mind, not the rules of the specific approach she had chosen.

This meant that she did not abandon the work. Instead, she improvised and changed what she was doing.

The result was a wonderful hybrid approach that she created in the moment. It was invented to meet the needs of that moment in a way that stayed true to the core requirements of memory reconsolidation.

At the end of the session, the client reported that the traumatic event resulted in no distress response at all.

CHAPTER 16

HOW TO KNOW
IF CHANGE HAS
OCCURRED

So far in this book, we have looked at what memory reconsolidation is and the steps needed for the brain to do it.

We have looked at ways of identifying the core predictions that need to be mismatched, and some possible approaches for creating a mismatch experience.

It is important to note that the approaches used are just examples of how to trigger memory reconsolidation. They are not memory reconsolidation itself.

Memory reconsolidation is the destination. The approaches, techniques and methodologies are merely the vehicles that get us there - so long as they follow the map.

There are likely an infinite number of approaches that can trigger memory reconsolidation.

But how do we check whether such change has occurred? How can you verify that memory reconsolidation has taken place as you hoped?

There are clear markers of change that distinguish memory reconsolidation from other kinds of improvement. Memory reconsolidation is not counteractive change. It does not leave the trauma intact with some additional new options.

Instead, it erases the trauma that you have been working on, so it is gone for good.

As such, change is not incremental. The client will not be a little better each time. They will not zig zag forward and back.

If memory reconsolidation has occurred, the change will be more sudden. Next time you see the client, the trauma response will be gone.

In this chapter, we will look at how to verify that this has occurred. There are typically three outcomes:

1. The trauma response is gone. The problem they were struggling with is no longer an issue.
2. The trauma response you were working on is gone. In its absence, verification reveals a separate trauma response that would still keep the problem alive.
3. The problem remains.

Outcome 1: Problem Solved

In the first instance, memory reconsolidation has taken place and the problem is resolved.

Outcome 2: Success and More to Do

In the second instance, memory reconsolidation has taken place, but there are other target learnings to address. This involves looping back and working with these remaining core predictions in the same way.

Many problems do have multiple targets. As such, memory reconsolidation can be successful and still leave some work to do on a separate target.

For instance, think of Jason, who stays in the background, missing opportunities in the process.

He senses that this is due to how his father criticised him as a young child. He doesn't want to step forward in life now, as his nervous system expects that same threat. Despite its many costs, it feels safer to stay in the background.

We may find that, since our attempt at memory reconsolidation, there has been a huge shift and the old fear of his father is gone. But there is something that still remains.

Exploring ultimately leads us to discover that, even without the criticism from his father, Jason fears being successful. His family expressed negative views about successful people, so to be successful risks rejection by those he most needs.

Notice how, with this client, we could discover that memory reconsolidation has worked without yet solving the problem.

The work we were doing with his father has been accomplished. Yet Jason's fear of being successful in life has not yet been addressed. It comes from a different target, and we need to loop back and work on this as a separate issue.

Outcome 3: No Memory Reconsolidation Took Place

In the third instance, it didn't work. So you need to keep going. Loop back to see if you had the right target learning. Maybe you need to generate a different mismatch experience to reconsolidate the trauma.

Before making a decision about which of these three outcomes occurred, we need to test if memory reconsolidation successfully took place or not.

Verification Work

When we verify memory reconsolidation work, we can use the information gathered during the opening stages of therapy.

You will recall that, when identifying the problem, we found some important information to help us move forward in our work.

We discovered:

- The problem itself
- Examples of how the problem shows up situationally
- How that feels in the body / nervous system in those moments
- What the desired outcome is instead
- How the problem situations would look different when our work is done

- How the nervous system mobilises against the client to stop them from getting their desired outcome

This information helps us during the verification phase of the work.

We already know what the client wants. We know their desired outcome and what that looks like. We know how their nervous system reacts in problem situations. We know how their nervous system reacts when they attempt to get what they want. We also have a collection of example scenes that trigger the client's problem.

We are able to use this information, amongst others, to check whether change has occurred.

Below is a road map of what to check in order to verify the success of your memory reconsolidation work:

1. Check the triggering situations where the problem shows up.

2. Check future imaginal scenes that would previously be triggering.

3. Check the activating scene that we used in the imaginal work.

4. Check other triggering scenes that have been mentioned during therapy.

5. Check the target learning explicit statement.

6. Check the desired outcome.

The Nervous System

In each of these six checkpoints, keep a special watch on the nervous system. The nervous system doesn't lie. Most of us can get temporary change with a little willpower. Think of how the gyms fill up every January as people briefly enact their New Year's Resolutions. Then check the same gyms in February to find them empty once more.

We are not looking for change that might involve willpower. Change that requires willpower implies that the barrier to change still exists, so we did our best to power through it.

The kind of change that occurs with memory reconsolidation is easy. Willpower is not needed. The trauma response that stood in the way of the change they want is gone. There is no need to power through. Indeed, there is nothing there anymore to power through.

By checking the nervous system responses, we are getting a truthful picture. The nervous system acts independently of us. When a scary part happens in a movie, you jump - except YOU don't jump at all. Your nervous system jumps you. It is a body hijack beyond your decision making.

These body hijacks are part of our inbuilt protection mechanism. They are predictions designed to keep us safe. But when they are based on outdated information, they need to be updated.

By checking the nervous system response directly, we are able to know whether the original core prediction is still active, or whether a new one has been successfully installed.

The easiest way to check the nervous system is by inviting the client to focus on what is happening in the body. As we make each of the six checks, we can ask the client to notice what bodily response occurs for them.

Much of this verification work is imaginal and experiential, as is a lot of memory reconsolidation work.

We don't want the client to logically think about a scene that would have previously been triggering. We want them to step into it, because this is more activating and will give us more evidence of its erasure.

The client will know very quickly whether:

A. It feels fine

B. There has been a shift but something still remains that needs more work

C. The old stuff is there as strong as ever

The Six Checks

Let's go through each of the six checks in detail:

1. Check the triggering situations where the problem shows up.

2. Check future imaginal scenes that would previously be triggering.

3. Check the activating scene that we used in the imaginal work.

4. Check other triggering scenes that have been mentioned during therapy.

5. Check the target learning explicit statement.

6. Check the desired outcome.

Problem Situations

In the opening sessions, we sought some examples of where the problem shows up and what it looks like.

For example, Reg struggles with boundaries. There are so many occasions that he wants to say no but doesn't. He feels anxious a lot of the time as he feels so out of control in life.

In the opening sessions he gave examples of when this shows up:

- At work when a colleague asks him to swap shifts

- At home when his partner decides on a vacation that he knows he will hate

- With friends when discussing the restaurant to eat at, and he stays silent despite having a clear preference

These are tangible examples of the problem as it showed up in Reg's life.

You can now experientially check in with these scenes. Ironically, I see my job here as attempting to prove that memory reconsolidation did NOT take place.

I am trying my best to activate the old triggers. It is only once I have fully tested them and gotten no response that I feel confident that it has successfully worked.

Likewise, if some other response is present and tied to a slightly different target, I want to catch that too. We can then work on that newly identified nervous system response going forward - as with Jason earlier.

We can use life itself to check how these situations have shown up since we last met.

Therapist: So Reg, I know that this problem would show up in a few places. People would ask you something and you wouldn't say no or state your own preference. Have you noticed yourself in any of those situations at all?

Reg: Yes. Mark asked me to swap shifts again and I didn't want to.

Therapist: How did it go?

Reg (matter of fact): I just told him no.

Therapist: You told him no? Wow. How was that for you?

Reg: It was easy. I didn't want to do it, so I said no.

Therapist: Okay, great. And what happened in your body as it was happening?

Reg: I was just calm. I didn't want to change shifts. I would have had to cancel badminton, so I just said no. I don't suppose I really thought about it.

Therapist: What about the butterflies that normally show up?

Reg: No, they weren't there.

Therapist: The weight in your chest?

Reg: No, it was fine.

Therapist: How about the blushing? You mentioned that you always blush during these things.

Reg (laughs): Yes, I actually didn't blush. Wow, I'd not realised that. But no, I didn't blush. I hate blushing. It feels like I'm showing my weakness. But no. No blushing.

Notice how Reg is very matter of fact. It's not a struggle. He's not powering through difficult feelings like a tug of war. It feels easy. This is a clear marker that memory reconsolidation has successfully occurred.

Notice too how checking on the nervous system responses uncovers evidence that can't be forced. People who blush try their very best not to blush. Yet that only makes it worse.

The absence of those involuntary nervous system responses, like blushing, is great evidence that memory reconsolidation has occurred.

Imagined Future Scenes

We can make similar checks using imaginal experiences. These involve inviting the client to be inside situations that would usually be triggering.

Therapist: So, has your wife talked about next year's vacation since we met?

Reg: No, that's not come up.

Therapist: Okay, so let's just fast forward to it coming up. Close your eyes and put yourself in that scene. There she is and she brings in a holiday brochure and starts telling you about the vacation she's thinking of. It's a vacation you really don't want to go on, the kind you'd hate. Be in it for a moment and notice what comes up.

Reg: It feels fine. I'm just thinking that I'm not going there.

Therapist: And are you saying that or just thinking it?

Reg: No, I'm saying it. I'm saying "I don't want to go there. I wouldn't enjoy that."

Therapist: And how is that for you? What's happening in your body? Check in with it a moment.

Reg: Yeah, it feels fine. I don't want to go, so I'm just telling her that.

Again, the client is immersed in a previously triggering scene that now has a "no big deal" quality to it.

The Imaginal Activating Scene

If you have done an imaginal reenactment of an old distressing scene, this is great source material. You can use that same scene to verify whether memory reconsolidation has taken place.

Simply invite the client to put their attention on the original distressing scene.

Therapist: So last time, we had a do-over of the scene with you and Dad.

Client: Yes.

Therapist: So, if you're ok to, just place your attention and your memory back on the scene as it originally happened. Notice what comes up for you as you place your attention there.

Client (after a short time): I'm not feeling anything, really.

Therapist: When you say you're not feeling anything, check in with yourself. Does that "not feeling anything" feel numb, or does it feel neutral?

Client: Yeah, it feels neutral. I mean, I'm looking at the original scene and I can remember it fine. But I don't feel any distress or anything like that.

Notice how the client feels no distress or nervous system responses, even when returning to the original, distressing event. In particular, see how the therapist checked to ensure that "not feeling anything" was neutrality rather than numbing.

Numbing is an autonomic nervous system response that would suggest there is more work to do. Neutrality is a lack of nervous system response to this scene, so is a sign that memory reconsolidation took place.

Other Triggering Scenes

At the start of therapy, you will have invited the client to share some situational examples of the problem.

As therapy continues, they will often share other triggering situations from their present-day life. For instance, they will describe a distressing situation that happened since you last met. Life has a habit of retriggering trauma responses, and so clients often talk about them with you.

You can collect these triggering scenes and, at the end of the work, test out their new nervous system responses to them.

Therapist: So, I'm remembering a time a few months back, when your boss unexpectedly called you in for a meeting. Do you remember?

Client: I'm not sure.

Therapist: It was morning around eleven, and suddenly you got an email saying she wanted to see you at three.

Client: Oh yes. I remember.

Therapist: Let's fast forward and imagine that happens again. Close your eyes and experience the uncertainty and the anticipation around that meeting. What comes up?

Client: Well, there's some worry there, I notice. I'm curious what she might want and if everything is okay. But I feel okay. I feel like I can hold that and just get on with my day.

Therapist: So this feels different from how it was last time?

Client: Oh yes, totally. I went to pieces last time. I couldn't do a thing until the meeting came.

Therapist: So how is this different as you experience that situation now?

Client: Well, I'm basically calm. I still have a bit of concern for what the meeting might be about. But I'm also curious too. Like maybe it's a good thing. So, I'm just carrying on and I'll find out when I find out.

Therapist: And that concern you feel - where would you say it belongs? How much of it is tied to how Mum was and how much feels present day? What's the percentage split?

Client: Oh no, it feels present day. My boss wants to see me and so there's some uncertainty and a bit of worry. It's different to how it was last time.

The Single Sentence and Other Explicit Statements

Another check is to re-introduce the Single Sentence Statement.

Earlier, we saw Vicki's core prediction stated as a single sentence:

If I reach out to my friends when I am feeling down

They won't respond because nobody truly cares about me

So I keep myself isolated in times of trouble

Even though I long to reach out and get support from my friends

Because ANYTHING is better than experiencing not being cared about.

We can show this to her now and ask her to notice whether it feels true. Note that we are not asking whether it is logically true, but whether it FEELS true in the body.

We use the Single Sentence to check her current allegiance to the statement that was at the heart of her core prediction.

Therapist: So, let's check in with your statement. Take a moment and just tell me if this FEELS true. Not neck up, but neck down. Don't ask your brain, check in with your body.

Vicki (laughs): No. To be honest, it looks ridiculous.

Therapist: It does?

Vicki: Yes. I don't believe any of that now.

This is a common response after memory reconsolidation. The thing that once felt so deeply true is now rejected.

The Desired Outcome

In the opening sessions of therapy, we invite the client to describe why they have decided to work with us. They typically describe the problem they want to deal with.

As mentioned earlier, I like to invite the client to describe their desired outcome. How will they know our work has been a success? What would they like to be happening in those moments instead?

Vicki may say that she wants to be reaching out to friends when she is feeling blue.

During those opening sessions, I checked Vicki's nervous system responses when she imagines doing just that. Here is what she said originally:

Therapist: So put yourself in that situation briefly now. You're feeling rotten and you notice you'd love some emotional support from your friend. Imagine yourself reaching for your phone and calling her number.

Vicki: Ughh. No. I couldn't.

Therapist: What happens in your body when you think of doing that?

Vicki: I feel sick. My jaw tightens and my stomach flips.

Therapist: Keep checking your body. What else do you notice?

Vicki: I feel a tightness in my chest and everything goes tense.

Therapist: Ok, that makes sense. So your stomach flips, your jaw tightens, you feel sick, and your chest feels tight, and you notice a tension in your body generally?

Vicki: Yes, that's right.

This early description gave us important information. It showed us which bodily responses mobilise to prevent Vicki from getting what she wants.

I invite Vicki to revisit this same imaginal scene of reaching out to call her friend. This will tell us whether this previous response has now changed as a result of our attempts to trigger memory reconsolidation.

Therapist: So put yourself in that situation briefly now. You're feeling rotten and you notice you'd love some emotional support from a friend. Imagine yourself reaching for your phone and calling her number.

Vicki (after a short while): Yes, that feels fine.

Therapist: What's happening in your body as you imagine yourself doing that?

Vicki: Relief, really.

Therapist: Relief?

Vicki: Yeah. I'm needing to talk to someone and so I do. So it feels nice. Like a relief.

Notice that this is a completely different answer from when she started therapy. There is no longer a nervous system response mobilised against her. Memory reconsolidation has overwritten the old prediction of threat.

Summary

Verification is a deeply important part of memory reconsolidation work. We need to know whether memory reconsolidation has taken place. If it has, change will be effortless for the client, and the effects will be permanent. If it has not, we must loop back and see what additional reconsolidation work is needed.

Using these six checks gives us a chance to reactivate the old trauma response. If it is still there, it will show up.

We try to prove that memory reconsolidation did not take place. The hope is that the trauma response is no longer there. If it is, it will show itself quickly, so pull back and work more gently. Otherwise, keep trying to prove that the trauma response is still present. Let its absence demonstrate that it is not.

If memory reconsolidation has indeed taken place, then there will be two outcomes:

1. The problem is gone.
2. The trauma response you worked on is gone, but, like with Jason's fear of success, there is another target still to work on.

Some of these dialogues may seem too good to be true on first reading. But this is what it is like for clients who no longer have this trauma response.

Memory reconsolidation has removed that response, so it is no longer there. They are now living life as if the trauma had never occurred, even though they still recall the original events.

Think of having the same conversations with someone who never experienced that trauma at all. None of these conversations would seem outlandish with them.

When memory reconsolidation occurs for clients, they too are without that trauma response.

CHAPTER 17

IMAGINAL WORK –
A RECAP

In this section, we looked at the role of imaginal approaches in trauma response removal.

Benefits of Imaginal Work

The benefit of using the imagination this way is two-fold. It allows mismatch experiences to be actively created. This is quicker than waiting to spot mismatch experiences. Secondly, imaginal work is experiential. This provides a more direct route to nervous system responses.

Therapists have long used the imagination as a tool in therapy, and it has an evidence base of success.

Of course, it is not the only way to trigger memory reconsolidation. No way of working can ever make that claim. But it does provide a powerful and effective range of approaches.

Examples of Imaginal Approaches

There are many ways one can use the imagination to generate these kinds of mismatch experience. For example, The Rewind Technique, The Ideal Parent Figure Protocol, and Goran Hogberg's Four Way Processing – to name but a few.

When working with the imagination to create mismatch, we can use a triggering scene from recent life, or find a scene from the client's past history.

To discover a scene from past history, The Movie Technique is an effective method for finding scenes that feel pivotal to the client.

You can then use whatever imaginal approach you both feel is appropriate in order to generate a mismatch experience.

My Imaginal Reenactment Protocol

One such approach is my own Imaginal Reenactment Protocol. This is done over a series of sessions by:

- Harvesting old feelings.
- Identifying the opposite, wanted feelings.
- Building a new scene engineered to create those new feelings.
- Repeatedly experiencing the new scene within the imagination.

To be clear, while this protocol is very effective at removing trauma response permanently, it is only one way to achieve memory reconsolidation.

The fundamental equation of memory reconsolidation is ACTIVATE + MISMATCH + REPEAT = OVERWRITE. So long as your work follows these beats, you have room to innovate and improvise the specific process that gets you there.

Verification

Once memory reconsolidation has been attempted, it is essential to verify whether it was successful or not.

When doing so, we will either discover:

- That the problem is resolved

- The problem remains (no memory reconsolidation occurred)

- The response you worked on has successfully resolved, but there is a different trauma response that would still keep the problem alive.

This verification stage helps shape the nature of any future work together, or helps you both decide to bring therapy to a close.

The Nervous System as a Guide

The nervous system is an essential guide, given that its responses are autonomic. For this reason, always enquire about nervous system responses which show up in the body.

Summary

You now know:

- How to identify a useful scene that reactivates the old trauma response.

- How to create effective imaginal mismatch experiences.

- How to check whether your work together has been successful.

CHAPTER 18

CONCLUSION

The discovery of memory reconsolidation has one key implication for therapists and our clients. Trauma response is no longer something to manage. It is something to be removed.

Solutions that require our clients to engage in life long exercises to keep trauma at bay are not transformational. They can help in the short term while the real work of therapy is being done, but are ultimately insufficient.

Memory reconsolidation shows that the brain already has a mechanism for removing trauma. It makes sense to use it.

When we do so successfully, the trauma response is gone and needs no managing. The change is permanent and the client needs no effort to keep those changes.

As therapists, we need to know which therapeutic interventions are counteractive (keeps the trauma) and which trigger memory reconsolidation (erases the trauma). The differences can be subtle in practice, yet have huge differences in effect.

In this book, we have looked at three aspects of memory reconsolidation:

- The discovery itself
- The seven steps of transformational change
- Using imaginal approaches

The Discovery Itself

In this section, we explored the neuroscientific breakthrough of memory reconsolidation. Neuroscientists have identified a brain mechanism that overwrites trauma responses and so removes them. This discovery was replicated many times in the experiments that followed.

It is the only known brain mechanism capable of doing so. It follows that anyone who has experienced trauma response removal has somehow triggered memory reconsolidation.

This marks a change from what neuroscientists had hitherto believed. Until then, it was believed that trauma responses were locked in to our brain pathways for good and could never be changed. As such, the goal of therapy was limited to creating and nurturing healthy responses in competing brain pathways.

When doing our work, we need to be aware of whether we are merely nurturing new brain pathways or overwriting the trauma response pathway.

Competitive therapy does result in change, but is always prone to relapse because it keeps the trauma response intact. Erasure therapy overwrites it, much like overwriting a cassette tape.

As a result, relapse is no longer possible. Likewise, exercises to keep trauma responses at bay are no longer needed. The trauma response is gone.

The overwrite does not remove the memory of what happened. It only overwrites implicit memory. When we trigger memory reconsolidation for our clients, they will still know what happened – but it will remove the distress.

Clients will say things like: "When I think of it, I can see that it's something that one might feel distressed by, but I'm not feeling any distress."

Likewise, the meanings, nervous system responses, and emotional responses associated with those events are gone too. Changes occur on a nervous system level. For instance, clients who blush in situations that resemble the trauma no longer do.

The Seven Steps of Transformational Change

Neuroscientists didn't just identify the fact of memory reconsolidation. They laid out the steps to take in order to trigger it. This means that therapists have a road map for our work.

The therapist Bruce Ecker identified seven steps, which he divided into three stages of a therapist's work (ABC-123-V):

- Prepare (ABC)
- Implement (123)
- Verify (V)

Preparation

He labelled the steps of the preparation stage as ABC:

A. Identify the problem.

B. Identify the target learning (or core prediction).

C. Identify mismatch experiences.

The core stance of this part of the work is that the client's problem makes sense. The aim is to discover how.

Why has the client not resolved the issue themselves? There is a prediction of a greater suffering if they do. They carry a prediction that says: If you get what you want, it will be even worse for you.

Like the man with the monster in the corridor, what may seem irrational turns out to be perfectly rational and protective.

To update such a prediction, we need to identify or generate mismatch experiences. These mismatch experiences may be discovered by:

- Asking about opposite life experiences, e.g. "So, tell me about a time when you did feel cared for."

- Being alert to mismatches as the client talks about their life.

- Creating mismatches through imaginal work.

Implementation

Ecker labelled the implementation stage as 123:

1. Activate the target learning (the core prediction that triggers the distress)
2. Activate the mismatch experience
3. Repeat

Memory reconsolidation occurs when there is a prediction error that is repeated.

The equation I use is ACTIVATE + MISMATCH + REPEAT = OVERWRITE.

When the brain's autopilot prediction is disconfirmed, the brain opens the relevant brain pathway for potential rewrite.

For instance, a client who simultaneously holds two contradicting "truths" will be in the midst of a mismatch experience.

Likewise, a person doing an imaginal reenactment that disconfirms the nervous system's expectations is also having a mismatch experience.

When we hold the old truth and the mismatch experience together at the same time, the brain pathway becomes rewritable. The door of the combination safe swings open, its contents ready to be replaced.

Earlier, we saw the metaphor of a game of conkers, where one conker is the old target learning and the new conker is the mismatch. Gently repeating the coming together of these two conkers is what updates the brain pathway with new learning, as we bring the old truth and the new truth together repeatedly.

When we do so successfully, the old trauma responses and their meanings are overwritten.

As such, therapists need to ensure that we:

- Hunt for or create mismatch experiences.
- Explicitly join the dots to connect the old truth to the mismatch.
- Repeat the game of conkers.

Verification

Once memory reconsolidation has been attempted, we need to make sure that it was successful.

This is an important part of the work. It allows us to find evidence that trauma response removal has taken place.

More importantly, it helps us notice when it has not taken place – or where success nonetheless leaves more work to be done.

Using Imaginal Approaches

Imaginal approaches have long been used by therapists as a resource in the therapeutic process. Such approaches work directly with implicit memory and have a good evidence base.

For instance, the Ideal Parent Figure Protocol, Goran Hogberg's Four Way Processing, and The Rewind Technique have all documented impressive results using imaginal methods.

A key benefit of imaginal work is that we can create mismatch experiences. This can save a lot of time in therapy. We can move into transformational work more quickly because we don't have to hunt for mismatches or wait for them to show up.

I outlined The Imaginal Reenactment Protocol I created. This covers four steps:

- Harvest old feelings
- Identify opposite feelings
- Build a new scene
- Experience the new scene imaginally

Closing Thoughts

Remember that any approach that meets the requirements of memory reconsolidation is not itself memory reconsolidation. It is important to separate the journey from the destination.

Memory reconsolidation is the brain mechanism that, when triggered, overwrites trauma response. This is the destination of therapy work.

The approach we take is merely the journey and vehicles that get us there.

The methods to discover the target learning and identify mismatches can be manifold. Similarly, there is likely an infinite number of approaches we can use to trigger memory reconsolidation.

The key formula is ACTIVATE + MISMATCH + REPEAT = OVERWRITE.

Whether using conversation or imagination (or something else entirely), so long as you are following this equation, you will give the brain what it needs to make transformational change.

Therapists and clients have the freedom to improvise and be creative in our work together. It also gives us the road map that allows us to tweak current approaches so that they, too, can trigger memory reconsolidation.

Since I discovered memory reconsolidation and tailored my work towards triggering it, it has changed my practice and the results I get with my clients.

It always pained me to hand people the additional burden of routines and exercises to keep their distress and trauma at bay. I longed for a better way, where they were simply free of it for good.

Memory reconsolidation is that way. When clients visit us seeking to overcome psychological injuries that still touch their life, we can now offer permanent transformation.

Every client brings not just their history, their problem, and their hopes. They bring with them a brain mechanism already capable of removing their own distress.

We now have the tools and the road map to engage that brain mechanism. Our role is to follow the steps of memory reconsolidation so the client can successfully trigger this in-built healing mechanism.

When we do, the results are astounding and sudden. They free the person from their trauma responses for good.

When you experience the results that memory reconsolidation brings for the people you work with, there is little in life so fulfilling. Good luck and have fun.

What Next

I have created a range of additional resources to help you remember and apply this book in your client work. To get these bonus resources, visit removetrauma.com

To read lots of free articles on this topic, visit FRESHTherapists.com where you can be trained by me personally.

You can also sign up to my FRESHTherapists newsletter to hear first about new articles and trainings.

You may like to join my Memory Reconsolidation Coaching Academy. This is exclusively for therapists and coaches who wish to be experts at removing trauma. You can find out more at FRESHTherapists.com/coaching

You can contact me directly at info@alunparry.com – I would genuinely love to hear from you. Get in touch knowing that your message will be welcomed.

Thank you for reading this book. I hope that it proves useful for you and your clients.

APPENDIX

FURTHER READING

FRESHTherapists.com – My website on all things memory reconsolidation.

Unlocking The Emotional Brain: Eliminating Symptoms At Their Roots Using Memory Reconsolidation by Bruce Ecker, Laurel Hulley and Robin Ticic.

Clinical Translation of Memory Reconsolidation Research by Bruce Ecker, International Journal of Neuropsychotherapy (June 2018). https://www.coherencetherapy.org/files/ Ecker_2018_Clinical_Translation_of_Memory_Reconsolidation _Research.pdf

Ideal Parent Figure method in the treatment of complex post traumatic stress disorder related to childhood trauma: a pilot study by Federico Parra, Carol George, Khalid Kalalou and Dominique Januel https://www.ncbi.nlm.nih.gov/pmc/ articles/PMC5700488/)

Affective psychotherapy in post-traumatic reactions guided by affective neuroscience: memory reconsolidation and play by Goran Hogberg, Davide Nardo, Tore Hallstrom and Marco Pagani. https://www.ncbi.nlm.nih.gov/pmc/articles/PMC3218787/

The effectiveness of Human Givens Rewind treatment for trauma by Shona Adams and Steven Allen, Mental Health Review Journal, August 2019. https://www.researchgate.net/publication/338198131_The_effectiveness_of_Human_Givens_Rewind_treatment_for_trauma

Muss' Rewind treatment for trauma: description and multi-site pilot study by Shona Adams and Steven Allen, Journal of Mental Health, October 2018. https://pubmed.ncbi.nlm.nih.gov/30346217/